SOULS

who leave us

12 True Stories from the Afterlife

Marie Johanne Croteau-Meurois

FOREWORD BY DANIEL MEUROIS

SOULS
who leave us

12 True Stories from the Afterlife

SACRED WORLDS
PUBLISHING

Souls who leave us – 12 True Stories from the Afterlife

Original French title: *Ces âmes qui nous quittent – 12 recits véridiques de l'Au-delà*

© 2017 Editions Le Passe-Monde
Author: Marie Johanne Croteau-Meurois

© 2019 Sacred Worlds Publishing for the English edition
www.sacredworldspublishing.com

The moral rights of the author have been asserted.

Translated by: Isabelle Laak.
Editing: Catherine Hensley
Cover Art: Adaptation of an artwork by Vincent Pompetti
Book Production: Aspen Oracle

2019 ISBN: 978-0-9987417-2-7

For Jacobée, my sister, beyond the millennia and forever,
For Virginia, who has courageously gone
through a great ordeal,
To the beautiful sensitivity of Julien, my son,
To my father, on the Other Side, and to my mother
already on the way to join him,

Then as a promise to Catherine with sapphire eyes,
To all those who have lost loved ones and are still
struggling with these departures,
To all those souls who asked me to tell their stories,
and to those I always help,
To all victims of barbaric and cruel acts,
To the healing of wounds, the ultimate goal,

To Daniel, my love of yesterday, today, and tomorrow,
For his patience, his love, and his editing,
To my friends and my students who also support me
and trust me,
Here are twelve stories, like a balm laid on sorrow.

A very big thank you to my painter friends who have graciously allowed me to reproduce their works, some of which were specially created for my testimonials: Annie Lautner, Christopher Saulière, Vincent Pompetri, and Marie-Chantal Martineau.

Annie Lautner: annie-lautner.com
Christopher Saulière: christophesauliere.com
Vincent Pompetri: pompetti.wordpress.com
Marie-Chantal Martineau: dauphinblanc.com

Table of Contents

Foreword 1

Introduction 5

The Beyond and its Dwellings 9

Chapter I : The Choice of Simone 21

Chapter II : A Black Rose 31

Chapter III : Emma's Story 47

Chapter IV : Cindy 69

Chapter V : The Little Rebel 77

Chapter VI : A Comeback 105

Chapter VII : The Cocoon 113

Chapter VIII : Pregnancy Time 119

Chapter IX : His Name was Francesco 129

Chapter X : I Don't Want to Die! 137

Chapter XI : Five Months and Then Nothing 145

Chapter XII : An Autumn Evening in Vancouver 151

Chapter XIII : The Day My Heart Stopped 163

Chapter XIV : The Importance of Being Able to Talk
about Your Own Death 171

Chapter XV : How Do You Envision Your Own Death
and What Comes After? 175

Notes and References 229

Glossary 235

End Notes 237

Also By 243

Foreword

I remember thinking for a moment when my wife asked me to write the foreword to the new book she was writing. Was it indeed a good idea? Did our proximity make me the best person for that? Not to mention the derogatory comments that this could provoke. Everyone can imagine them.

And then the idea made its way. Why not, indeed? Was I not the right person for such an exercise? Was I not in the best position to talk about the authenticity and intensity of her life experience in a field where—it must be acknowledged—many people think they grasp it without any experience or worthy research?

What makes Marie Johanne so unique is that she is hypersensitive[1] and has a high sensitivity, two essential qualities in a field as delicate as the one of death and accompanying the ones who leave us. These qualities, along with her spontaneity, her simplicity, and her integrity, make her a direct witness, an experimenter who has something to say on the subject without going through the filters of psychology, parapsychology, beliefs, religions, and superstitions.

But beyond all that, what deserves to be highlighted is the work of helping the suffering souls that she accomplishes, to which this book is the testament.

Souls Who Leave Us is certainly not just a collection of stories about the Afterlife. As you read it, you will experience very quickly the diffusing of a healing blast. Marie Johanne has toned down suffering situations and planted seeds of hope—a

1

hope our world, in its increasing toughness and cynicism, is terribly lacking.

To do this, the book is presented as a basis for reflection accessible to all of us. It is addressed directly to the heart with the coherence and freshness of the soul inherent to "the one who lives" who does not worry about the often cruel and "disconnected" analysis of the intellect.

Reading the testimonies reported in this book, some may be tempted to say they "already knew all this," but knowing is surely not being aware and even less necessarily understanding. We can regularly notice this during exchanges on the issue.

This is why I am convinced that makes the force of *Souls Who Leave Us* what I have named "the heart wave," meaning the truth and kindness in the pages builds gradually to a magical sense of teaching and subtle transmutation, without a doubt supporting more than we can realize.

In fact, Marie Johanne tenderly induces the urgent need to look differently not only at the phenomenon of death and its approach but also even more at the importance given to the quality and essence of daily life. Because your "after" will logically be the image of your "before," this will determine your "during."

What is very surprising is the deliberate action—we should say congenital—of Western society to avoid everything related to death. It's as if all its active members have decided to block any real free reflection on the subject. Is it fear of the truth and what it would imply as a reform—a metamorphosis of consciousness and, consequently, behavior? Yes, without any doubt.

So we must repeat, repeat, and multiply the testimonies until immersion, until a kind of collective cerebral shell cracks and finally loosens in a salutary movement.

This book offers detailed cases of difficult deaths and souls lost in crossover due to being deeply wounded, as many are. These lost souls are very special to their loved ones, who need to know that they are finally "safe" by returning to the Light.

It does not carry great revelations but affirms its intention to touch the heart, the true human heart, simply and spontaneously, the heart that is the essence of everything beautiful and uplifting.

This is the richness of the book to which readers will be sensitive, perhaps silently but in depth, far from the conditioning of theories or "speculations."

At no time do the stories that compose the book affirm "I know" but instead allow all to understand "I have experienced it."

This is its strength.

Daniel Meurois

Introduction

I remember my birth very well. I mean "my birth" as first being in the womb of my mother and then the second one, the one of my delivery to Earth. Coming into the world from the terror of the woman who is carrying you is very difficult.

This "no welcome" of my mother was a great ordeal for the small soul I was and not really desired. Imagine a little being who wants to grow in her mother's womb, a little being the mother is scared of and repelled by.

One feels everything when one is an embryo and then a fetus. Yes, absolutely everything! My mother couldn't control her fear because a doctor had told her that she could never give birth. Fortunately, the love of my father helped and carried me with strength. My father was my genitor but also a "virtual uterus" with his comforting presence and big, loving hands that I felt through the flesh of my mother's belly when she cried while fearing that I was some kind of monster. Thank you, Dad!

Everything is still so alive and painful in my memory that I can hardly relive the images to describe them. I keep deep wounds in my heart. Yes, I can still hear the cries of my mother, the panic of the doctor and the anesthetist, and the violence of the metal rods forcing me to go to an "outside" that terrified me.

Finally, there was a muffled and dry sound, an intense cold, an odor of iodine mixed with blood, a blinding light, and a gliding of my head into a metal-shaped bean. Then I was briefly introduced by the nurse, who was holding me in one of her hands, to my father, who was anxiously waiting in the corridor.

With a tiny and translucent body, I appeared, two huge blue eyes wide open, staring at him intensely. Then there were forty days spent trying to survive in an incubator. Here is the terrestrial welcome that was reserved for me.

Indeed, I was born prematurely at seven months of gestation with symbols on my skin that some traditions say announce the arrival of a *particular* soul, a soul with a gift.

I had the placental veil on my head and, on my left hand, an outline of the Star of David. I did not learn the meaning of these signs until much later, from a great medium of the 1980s, Alex Tanous, who is now deceased.

At the age of two, I was assailed by a long and intense fever for seven days. When they finally found the origin of the sickness, I was operated on urgently. My exhausted young heart, as I was told later, had stopped for a minute or more on the operating table until they managed to revive it. The doctor only informed my father that there had been some complications during the surgical intervention, that my heart had suffered but that everything had gone well. Finally, he added, "She is not big, your little girl, but she is resilient! Have her baptized quickly. We never know, because the next days will be critical."

I was baptized the next day in the afternoon without the presence of my mother. My maternal grandparents were named as my godparents. I was still hospitalized. After the baptism, I was returned to my glass cage to finish my extrauterine gestation. It was an artificial place, well-heated certainly but without maternal warmth.

What can this little girl share about what she saw and experienced on the Other Side during her short NDE[2]?

Nothing. But much later, the experience of her brief "return to the Light" surely enabled her to refine this special gift and her love for Christ and the angels.

Christ was indeed my imaginary friend throughout my childhood, according to the interpretation chosen by my parents. (They'd smile while talking about it because they were not really believers.) Today, Christ is still present in my life and very alive in my heart, although He is not the one from the churches.

The stories in this book are real testimonies. My particularity is that I am a "Helper Soul."[3]

I help souls in difficulty on the "Other Side of the Veil." I meet with the dead ones.

The cases mentioned in these pages are purely authentic. I would like it to be known that I have recounted them with infinite respect for those involved since they left this Earth too abruptly. Each soul requested a testimonial for his or her family.

I do not want to convince readers "at any price." However, I feel strongly in my soul and awareness that, for the families, reading these stories will help to heal misunderstandings about their loved ones who are gone. Therefore, even beyond time, these souls will have received justice.

Helping, healing, and loving—my only way.

Marie Johanne Croteau-Meurois

The Beyond and its Dwellings

First and Foremost, an Overview

I've practiced aid to the Passage for many years. Quite simply, it is a gift. It's also a faculty that I have sometimes refused, because "*talking with spirits*" puts me in a state of great fragility.

I have always been extremely sensitive and porous to the subtle energies, from the smallest to the heaviest. From the beginning, I knew that this way would not be easy and that it would be denigrated by a crowd of skeptics. I have finally understood that because I received this faculty at birth, this gift to listen to and see the dead, it was a gift from the "Intelligence of Life" to not only help deceased souls but also their distraught relatives.

As far as I am concerned, I've chosen to come to the aid of souls who could not find the Light and were "wandering." I am referring to the souls of those who committed suicide; of those who experienced violent deaths or left in a state of loneliness; of those who were victims of homicide, collectively or individually; and of those who were aborted.

Of course, I also accompany souls who need help in the Afterlife after long illnesses and those who ask for help for one reason or another.

I occasionally participate with other Helpers and help the flights of deceased souls who die suddenly in a group without understanding what's happening, like those in the

Bataclan theater in Paris, at the Promenade des Anglais in Nice, or during the Christmas market in Germany, to name a few among the most recent mass murders. Depending on the cases, I go to them or they come to me. I don't always decide because sometimes it's an Afterlife guide who introduces them to me, or the family of the deceased asks me to intervene when they feel the soul may be in difficulty. As we will see later, I help the ones who leave us to understand and most of all accept that they are "dead" on Earth but still alive in another way, in another world, similar to a new country. This is my commitment of service.

The World of the Dead

But first, very briefly and before inviting you to travel, let's see what these worlds are, these many other living spaces that, on the Other Side of the Veil, welcome those who leave us.

For the souls, what are these worlds that open wildly in front of them? Are they invitations to affirm that death is not really an end but rather a transition, a passage toward "something else," where a soul evolves under different conditions until a future incarnation?

How can I express these questions to you and try to answer them? Because I have direct experience in the Afterlife helping so many souls, and I come back alive.

How can I do that? Because of my natural ability to discorporate myself—in other words, my ability to project my consciousness out of my body—I manage to cross the "Great Door" in a kind of round-trip. My subtle body travels between the worlds.

Am I "strange" or, worse, crazy? I am not alone in having this gift, because testimonials are now popping up everywhere! In the old days, the risk of triggering judgments made me scared and, most of all, very hurt.

Now it makes me smile because I'm not looking for anything. I have nothing to prove. I talk about what I am experiencing, and it feels good to anyone who hears it. To move forward in expanding consciousness and growing up, we must not listen to skeptics who, by always denying everything, shrink life and remove hope. I call them "wing-burners."

Systematically denying the phenomena that sometimes shake up daily life has never changed anyone. On the contrary, this makes one regress through confinement in a state of mind that is ultimately often quite painful. Of course, no one will ever be able to change a skeptic's mind because he or she is looking for scientific validation according to current rigorous standards and wants to measure what cannot be measured. Therefore, it is necessary to change the parameters! More than proof by a + b, it is experience that can disrupt everything.

What is nonetheless surprising is that our current society, which is moving to be more and more intangible with all the digital and virtual gadgets, artificial intelligence, and special effects of science fiction movies, rejects the possibility of the existence of parallel worlds, especially one that could bear the name "Afterlife."

The intangible and tangible have never been so present in our lives, and yet our collective consciousness continues to cling to a uniquely dense and monolithic vision of the universe.

Is it not a remarkable incoherence? Nothing can exist outside of our world, neither before nor after, or in outer space, or on the Other Side? The Afterlife is a pipe dream? And the soul in all this? Does it exist?

The Soul

Yes, it does exist. By the way, what do you think the soul is? Does it have a weight? Is it made of quantifiable matter in a body of flesh and bone? Who has never asked these questions? The ocean of the soul is vast.

Have you ever *really* accompanied a dying person in the last days of life? If so, did they not confide in you that they had strange perceptions, like seeing a dead person?

11

Then you thought maybe they were having delusions due to their medications or hallucinations related to their condition. No. We will see that these are real and authentic perceptions.

Someone who is said to be "at the end of life" is already half in another world, in a new life.

Almost always, a few hours after death, a soul moves constantly back and forth between our world and "the Other Side of the Veil." They perceive the presence of people who were dear to them, those who died before them. These other souls are there to "fetch" the newly arrived soul.

The soul also observes the active presence of the Guides of the Passage, who will assist with the birth into "Heaven," just as they were present at the time of birth on Earth.

Did you know that there can be this many people in a room with a dying man and that he perceives them as much he hears you?

Birth into the Other Side of the Veil

Does the person who just died live on the Other Side? Actually, he finds himself on the Other Side in the same state he was in when he left his earthly life. If you die in revolt, you "wake up" in revolt, and still alive—but in life *differently*, meaning in your Body of Light, the one that we sometimes call the "astral body."

So, you leave with your last concerns and worries, those that have followed you in life—absences, mistakes, lies, actions, abandonment, and also, of course, aspirations. She keeps in herself her conditioning, her potential, and everything that contributes to her own level of consciousness. She then rebuilds her surroundings and her routine, similar to finding a space that is familiar to her, marked by her boundaries.

This is how a birth into Heaven happens with a new body, one not of flesh but of a subtle and luminous energy. This is simple and fluid, or at least it should be. It happens, however, that a body may be convinced it is damaged or under the influence of drugs. There are for these cases "hospitals" of pyramidal or ovoid shape dedicated to such transitions. The body of the soul is treated, readjusted, and regenerated by "doctors" of the Afterlife.

The Void?

If a soul considers nothing but a void as following death, she will find the same nothingness in the Afterlife. She will have built the void, since she will have believed in it throughout her life of flesh because of her lack of hope. In other words, in life she was not able to increase the rhythm of her fundamental vibration, what I call the "perfume" or "color of the soul." Following death, she will find herself stuck in this nothingness. She will remain in it until she opens her inner eyes to her own light, because every soul has, despite everything, a small flame of the Presence Divine inside—every soul without exception!

In summary, each person must overcome the barriers or parameters that his or her culture, religious beliefs, or atheism set in place. The higher the level of consciousness of the being, the easier it is to transition.

The Problem of Attachment

Some souls refuse the Light because they are too tied to the earth. They have multiple enslavements and unfulfilled desires. These souls usually wander in a space very close to that of terrestrial life, a heavy and dense space commonly referred to as the "Lower Astral."

From this vibratory zone, they sometimes disturb the people they loved or the places where they suffered and created multiple powerful links. They are what we call "zombies" or "lost souls." Their lives, then, continue in an etheric space from which they try to intervene in our physical plane and draw attention. In search of an issue, they call for help. Such a soul is in a mental prison and does not see the Door.

Of course, when I speak of these souls, I do not speak of life-forms marked by darkness. I do not want to develop such a subject here, which is too creepy in my opinion to appear in these pages that are intended to foster understanding and hope.

Generally speaking, a soul confronted with the problem of attachment continues to reproduce the same gestures and accomplish the same courses of action until a walker or guide prompts them to "wake up" and enter a vibratory space of hope and, therefore, light.

This is quite often the case for someone who died violently.

I have seen that the suddenness of such a departure makes it easy to believe that the person is still alive among us.

She can then go through a state of confusion and incomprehension in the face of what she sees "around" her when she feels alive and well near us but we do not see her. It is obviously for her very difficult to have the proximity to a world she still wants to be hers and continues to see but in which she cannot intervene anymore. She ends up asking, more or less consciously, for some help. I've noticed that it is roughly the same for a death by homicide. The difference is that such an experience can engender a long attachment to the earth when it is fueled by a desire for revenge.

In all cases, it is at this precise moment that, with the acceptance of aid, a soul can really be supported up to a certain point by the walkers or guides. The soul will then be invited to various transition levels, starting with the closest to their level of understanding, before they can progress to brighter spaces. They are always guided and accompanied.

But the phenomenon of attachment does not only lead to the space of the Lower Astral. It also leads to a vibratory universe sometimes called the "Kamaloca," which corresponds, if you prefer, to the famous purgatory of the Christians.

The Three Levels of the Kamaloca

First Level

This is a zone of "no-being," a dark space where the soul is confronted by her own fears and the realities of low vibration. It is sometimes a zone of midconsciousness, even sleep. Guides of the Light work there to stimulate and pacify what needs to be taken care of.

Second Level

This is the one I mentioned earlier, where some souls are blocked between two vibratory worlds because they cannot detach themselves from the material world. I have noticed that the attachment is often nourished by guilty feelings, lack of love, or even low self-esteem. Alzheimer's disease can be one of the causes of a very punctual stay in such a mental space.

The walls of the "dwelling place" made by one of these souls remain sealed until the soul perceives of the absurdity of the horizons they've created, which leads to a kind of saturation and indicates the existence of an "energy lock" to a higher altitude and light. It is at this time that the intervention of a Helper between the worlds will be very useful. A dialogue between the Helper and the suffering soul will enable the opening of a door toward the Light, where other Guides take over. This work can be long or brief, depending on the opening ability of the being. I will have the opportunity to talk more about this with the stories in this book and will deepen the overview of the levels of the Kamaloca.

Third Level

This area is called specifically the "Kamaloca" (in the fullest sense) by Asians. It is a space where souls reproduce their terrestrial functioning schemas with all their limitations. In this state, they are not necessarily aware of "having crossed the border" or going around in circles tirelessly. It is also in this vibratory zone that souls have the opportunity to review their lives in order to take stock and then move on.

Most people go through this space of transition. The few who avoid this vibrational zone, the Kamaloca, have higher aspirations not tied to beliefs or religion, whatever it may be. These higher aspirations are rooted in a clearness of consciousness.

Fitting for this subject is an excerpt from the book There Are Many Dwelling Places by Daniel Meurois[4], which summarizes the Kamaloca pretty well:

"By using the expression 'dimensions of purgatory,' I am not referring to its extent or area, geographically speaking. The worlds of the souls cannot be understood or even located in the traditional sense because they expand or retract— precisely—according to the souls that create them, inhabit them, and evolve there. I have noticed that this great vibratory manifestation called Kamaloca is particularly significant in this respect because its primary character is that of instability. It cannot be otherwise because the souls who enter it maintain the same existence and experience, fluctuating with unsatisfactory values. It is the world of enslavement to the creases of the soul, to her insatiable appetites and her drowsiness. It is also the world where people are trying to understand their frustrations.... It must be understood that these states are not states of suffering but rather 'stationary areas.' The soul runs in circles around itself. By creating situations that, a priori, suit her, she is confined to a certain level of vibration. She limits herself, feeling that there is an 'elsewhere' or 'otherwise' that she cannot reach. A kind of dissatisfaction and nostalgia catches up to her sooner or later, similar to what she felt on Earth but with fewer obstacles, because she blocks the manifestation. In reality, this dissatisfaction is saving her. It is indeed from her that the impulse of life will come, the momentum of transformation likely to push the being to break the cocoon in which she had taken refuge before enclosing herself there."

With this excerpt, we can better understand the fact that purgatory is not a place but an illusory psychic state related to the transition period a soul is in. There are as many purgatories as spaces of sensibility.

It is an area of purification and also security that allows the soul to do, at its own level of consciousness, an examination of itself before being able to perform a high jump to more light.

Most of the souls that make up our humanity still live in a kind of half-light of consciousness. Under such conditions, it is logical that what a soul has been lacking follows her to another world.

It is very important to understand that a soul does not necessarily go through all of these states, which are, in fact, only the result of a number of mental and emotional constructs. This is where one realizes that it is important in life to "work on yourself," to lead a healthy life in all respects, especially loving and maintaining positive thoughts. You can lie to everyone and about everything, but not to yourself.

A Particular Case: The Suicide

After this general overview, the issue of suicide emerges. What happens to the ones who commit suicide? Personally, I have always seen them first pulled by the lowest layers of the vibratory zone of the Kamaloca—in other words, the Lower Astral.

It must be stated that this is not a space of punishment but rather understanding, where the deceased is helped with their internal path. The soul inevitably experiences pains and revolts until they learn to consider these differently as "learning phases."

Even when "dead," you travel with your emotional and mental baggage. We must realize the consequences. Suicide does not solve anything. Each suicide, though, is a unique case. It is not our responsibility to judge.

Does Hell Exist?

Yes and no. Hell is nothing more than a holographic bubble darker than all those of the Kamaloca. Let us see it as a virtual dungeon a soul locks herself in because of the baseness of what she has allowed to seep into it. As such, this virtual psychic space is not eternal, contrary to what religion claims. The Light enters sooner or later by visiting the dark areas to invite the suffering soul to enter a state of brighter consciousness, hope, and restoration.

It is important to remember that it is always the degree of consciousness, detachment, and actual elevation of a soul that determines its trajectory. To understand the phenomenon of death and its forms is to understand that wanderings after crossover do not continue indefinitely.

The Passage

After a stay in the different areas of the Kamaloca, a soul is finally invited by their own internal state to go through another doorway. It will be their possible ascension to what is called the "Devachan." This universe will reveal itself totally in agreement with their deep aspirations, their ideal. It is useful to specify, then, that the Devachan is also the vibratory result of a multitude of sensitivities, and so it is composed of many worlds.

What Is the Devachan?

It is a space that we can also call the "Middle Astral." It is constituted of a multitude of spheres of souls. It is the home where the being can finally find peace. He can live his own conception of what is called "Heaven."

A soul who has lived a second death in the Kamaloca is finally released here from his main mental divisions. Each enters into a real metamorphosis. It is a big step forward for them because they can redefine their skyline, their hopes, their needs for love, and they can rethink the subtle architecture of their new life. This means that they generate a new hologram, a new virtual world to the extent of what lives in them and what they have lived through in their incarnations. In the Devachan, every soul is in front her potential and make her dreams come true:

"The Devachan can be defined as the 'Sweet Home' of the soul who finds peace and happiness while continuing her path of refinement and transformation. We must not lose sight of the fact that this 'Heaven,' for as sweet as it is, remains itself a psychic construction. This means that it, too, is being transformed because it is continually modeled by consciousness in motion. Over the years, I have been amazed by the idea of Heaven held by so many of our contemporaries, those who believe in the Afterlife. Mostly, this idea is very childish, as infantile and fixed as the classic representation of God. What we call 'Heaven' is generally conceived of as a world of rest in the midst of idealized nature, a world where souls live an inactive, beatific way while meeting angelic presences—a vision of happiness that seems more a form of absolute tranquility than anything else. Let us understand that the different levels of manifestation of the Devachan—beyond the quietness they provide to souls— are at first worlds toward Awakening."[5]

It is therefore in this multifaceted world that the soul will continue to work on herself and thus participate in the infinite movement of life. She will evolve, learn according to her aspirations, and experience, taught by different teachers. With the Guides of Light dedicated to each soul, helping with the preparation for these next life incarnations, the soul will one day be able to detach from the cycle of incarnations and move toward the Light, another step of learning in the School of Life.

Chapter I

The Choice of Simone

"The one who loves, who loves without seeking or dominating or possessing, immediately becomes aware of the absolute unity of everything. He actualizes the poets' dreams; he makes direct experience from them. He gives birth to the One, God, in him."
— *Vu d'en Haut* (Seen from Above) by Daniel Meurois

Thinking of meeting Simone and all she brought to me being so rich in teachings, I would perhaps not be the person I am today without her. Some encounters are decisive. Though it may seem insignificant in the moment, it could be a proposition of life. Each rendezvous can be important, whether with a great master or not.

It is always in a moment of great simplicity and tenderness that the germ of an internal metamorphosis begins.

I was barely sixteen when I noticed Simone. I was a teenager then living through my very first existential revolts, and she was a neighbor, always smiling, with a look that I perceived as good in the true sense of the word. She was a mother of three, married, and infinitely discreet.

From the window of our dining room, I could not help but observe her regularly. I knew her long, pale, chestnut-colored hair, free in the sun, and her Madonna-like face were going to form a memory in me. Yes, Simone had that *something* in her that challenged the soul. She radiated "Heaven" and also shades of Mary the Virgin, someone she venerated very obviously in her living setting.

And as for the beautiful emerald green light that I perceived around her, her subtle presence questioned my own inner light. Since early childhood, I have always been able to see radiances around people. Much later, I learned that these were called "auras."

To tell you everything, at that time in my life I had lost what is called "faith," and my imaginary friend, from my childhood, had also left me.

To tell the truth, he had not left me. I was deaf to him. The courses of existential philosophy, the works of Albert Camus, Jean-Paul Sartre, and Friedrich Nietzsche, as well as the long hours of listening in my room to the songs of Léo Ferré, had me turned upside down, and I do not think that it was for the better.I had like a deep sorrow in my heart, a despair of the human as well as a nostalgia for the Sun. *"Man is an animal whose qualities are not yet fixed,"* Nietzche claimed.

Simone was also "attracted" to or intrigued by me. One summer day when I was lying in the sun with a book of philosophy, she spoke to me over the Siberian pea shrub hedge between our two suburban homes.

"Hello," she said joyfully. "This sun does us good, doesn't it? Tonight, some friends of mine are coming to my house, and I wanted to invite you. Are you available?"

Her big blue eyes were so tender and her smile more than disarming. It was wide, her smile, a bit like that of the American actress Julia Roberts. I was really surprised that a mother more than twice my age would invite me to her home with her friends.

"Me? But why?" I asked her. "We don't know each other at all, and I don't even know your friends. I will be uncomfortable… and embarrassed."

"I've organized a prayer meeting with healer women, and I think it will interest you. We help people who are suffering."

"Healers? Oh really? And why me?"

Her answer completely ignored my questioning, as if for her everything was self-evident.

"Good. I will count on you," she responded with her very special smile. "It starts at 8 p.m.!"

I do not know what pushed me to go there. It was such a strange invitation! I informed my parents that I was going to a friend's house for a few hours and that I would not be home too late. I did not want to tell them where I was going.

I was disturbed, intensely disturbed. Very anxious, I showed up at the agreed-upon time.

That evening, without me knowing it, Simone opened her "door" to a space that produced a big shock to my soul. I was immediately overcome by a slight dizziness when I walked in. It smelled of incense, and I loved this cozy atmosphere that expressed a certain "sacred" quality, precisely the quality that had tried to manifest itself more in me that I had left in dormancy since I was eight.

Simone quickly introduced me to some women already sitting in the living room. On the floor, there was a cotton mat, and someone was lying on a pale blue mohair blanket. She was a girl about my age, someone I had known from one of my classes a few years earlier. My eyes were immediately drawn to her right arm, which was encased in a plaster cast.

Simone explained to me very naturally that the young Ange-Marie had bone cancer and that together, with our prayers and our hands, we were going to try to help her heal. One of the "healer" women, who was Ange-Marie's mother, invited me to sit down close by her on the floor. All the other women sat in our wake, also around the sick girl.

I let myself be won over by the reaction, the opening of my soul, which exulted in the moment. It was obvious! She was *back home*. There were no words, no noise, simply an inner rosary of our prayers and the tenderness of our hands on the arm of Ange-Marie, Ange-Marie with her beautiful closed eyelids, calm, in gratitude.

Then came what I took for a miracle. I heard in me a male voice with a hoarse accent:

"Listen to me. Listen! What you must pray with is not your head but your heart. It is your heart that must recall 'the initial perfection' to the cells of Ange-Marie. The key is in the first atom, in the microcosm, initial perfection's holder. Thus occurs the healing. Remind the arm of its first reality without doubting."

I never repeated to anyone, especially not to my family, those words I heard that night. They remain timidly in the secret garden of my heart. Today, I release them so that they can also bloom in you. This "message" resonated so strongly in me on that strange evening that it marked my soul with a seal of "recovery," and it made me rediscover the beloved look of Master Jesus.

The voice I heard was as overwhelming as a message of "Get up and walk!" It is he who put me rightly back on the path to my true way of life, and now that the memory has returned to me, I dare say that 2,000 years ago I received from Him a prayer as a gift. I offer you here some lines:

"... Lord, lift me up and teach me the smile that speaks to those burdened by inner storms as well as those weighed down by tears. Enter the hollow of my hands so that the wounds of those who suffer can be healed by your name."[6]

The Choice

Deeply jostled by what I'd experienced, I did not attend other meetings that were organized at Simone's house. I needed to integrate everything that was open in me, or rather reopened.

I wanted to understand what happened. I also needed to take a step back. I informed Simone, who, although disappointed, respected my decision.

"If ever you wish to return, you will always be welcomed!" she said.

Simone and I continued to talk regularly about the people she was receiving in the healing circle. She had a patient, Louise, who was in her early forties and a mother of two children. Louise was separated from her husband and had recurrent breast cancer with metastases in the lungs. After several healing circle sessions, there had been no noticeable results. Louise sank into sadness despite the efforts of Simone and the chemotherapy treatments in parallel. She felt her death approaching and was terribly frightened, because for her, death meant falling into a big hole of nothingness. It was the absolute void!

A few days after our discussion about Louise, my neighbor entrusted me with something that really left me speechless. I could never have guessed there was such a huge and intimate suffering in this luminous woman. For her, everything seemed to always go so well. Never a complaint!

"Marie Johanne," she said, "I think you can hear what I am going to share with you. I can't tolerate my husband anymore. The odor of his body and soul has become unbearable.

He's a butcher, and his work has become unbearable for me, as a vegetarian. I cannot do it anymore! In some way, he is killing me. All that he is and all that he says produce in me an immense disgust. I've tried. Nothing helps, even when he puts his hands on me. I cannot stand him anymore. I cannot stand him anymore or his demands. I do not despise him, but I cannot live with him anymore. Now that the kids are big enough, I can leave."

"Oh? I do not believe my ears," I said. "You never let anything show to anyone! So, you are going to separate yourself from him?"

"No!"

"What are you going to do then?"

"I am taking Louise's place."

"What?" I exclaimed.

"Listen, I am not afraid to die. I know it and have often experienced it, again and again, and I know it doesn't exist. I am not going to leave my husband. I am going to take Louise's cancer *on me*. I am not attached to my life here. I am talking about my journey on Earth. I did my time to a great extent, while Louise...." Simone paused and closed her eyes. "Well, she wants to live! She will not heal. I saw it. Her husband left her. Her children are little. They still need their mother."

I was shocked.

"But you can't do it, Simone!" I said. "How can you take someone else's disease onto your own destiny?"

"By a soul pact between both of us."

"I don't believe you. I beg you to not say more stupid things."

"Don't worry. The 'exchange' is already happening. Soon, I will be in Louise's same state, and she will be healed and can continue her life with her children. As for me, I know what to expect, and it will be perfect like it is."

"But all of this is nonsense. You scare me!"

"Don't you worry. You will see that all will happen very fast. When it's completed and I've gone through the Passage, I will come back to give you a sign so you know that I am doing well. I promise. I love you!"

Of course, reading these lines, everyone will think that Simone was totally unbalanced and delirious, just like I felt at the time. But in fact, this kind of "exchange," though exceptional, can actually happen with evolved souls. I am not talking about spiritually accomplished masters but rather old souls who are ahead of others.

In the animal kingdom, this is also verified. Some animals can take on the sicknesses of their human masters and even die instead of them. I am certain that you have been witness to this phenomenon at least one time in your life without even realizing it. I would like to open another door to this subject with an excerpt from the book ***Le Peuple Animal (The Animal People: The Souls of Animals)***. Here is an animal who expressed itself with telepathy:

"Sometimes, the Spirit of Life who animates us will ask one of us to take a little bit of your sadness and this strange weight that you are carrying. This is kind of a door that opens, a sharing reflex, and the animal will absorb a bit of what is too heavy for your soul. Then, don't be surprised if a fever kills your pet, or horrific itches torture it, or it loses hair.

In these moments, there is something like a gray mud, a sticky substance that develops on the surface of the animal's spine. He or she can't help it. There is something in your heart that finds a logic to that. The bird-souls that live close by, in your houses, accept this suffering too, but most of the time, a bird-soul can't stay in its body. Only our cat brothers, you see, know how to heal themselves from your illnesses that they absorb."[7]

Of course in this case, this was an animal, but it is exactly this same process that can be created in humans. We can exchange unconditional and compassionate love.

The End

It was school holidays. Through my window, I watched Simone's hair in the sun. It had become dull, and she was visibly missing a few strands, as if she were losing them abundantly. I could no longer perceive her usual radiance. I told myself she had to be depressed with everything she was experiencing with her husband. In fact, I had almost forgotten what she'd told me, her famous and strange pact that, for me at the time, had no chance of actually being carried out.

One day, I went to go camping with a group of college friends. Simone was only a slight haze in my head. I was young, and I wanted to enjoy summer and the beautiful world that was around us.

With a carefree heart, I finally came back home to resume my studies. I remember it was one of those beautiful evenings at the end of August, one of those nights when the weather is so mild that there is not a single breath of wind. I was in my room, stretched out on my bed with a good book when, suddenly, the light white curtain of my nearby window brushed against me, as if the subtle wind had intentionally moved toward me in order for the cloth to reach me. At the same time, I felt a "presence" sitting at the end of my bed. The mattress was even slightly depressed. It was exactly 8 p.m.

Frightened, I intuitively whispered a first name, the only one that could come to me in such circumstances.

"Simone?" I said. "Is this you, Simone?"

Slowly, the silhouette of a woman appeared at the foot of my bed. She was made of a very pale blue vapor, and I saw her smile. There was also a slight rose scent that accompanied her. Simone loved roses so much!

"Yes, it's me," she said. "Do not be afraid. I came to tell you that I am fine. Tell it to my loved ones, to my children. I left so fast that they are disoriented."

Unable to hear anymore, I left my room quickly, totally in a panic, thinking at first I was the victim of hallucinations. I did not say anything to my parents, who were in the living room in front of the TV. But as I did not want to be alone, for fear of having another "hallucination," I sat down with them.

It was Simone's husband who informed my parents that his wife had passed away in a hospital in Quebec. We didn't even know that she had been hospitalized! It was a shock for us, and you can imagine my sorrow.

Not too long after Simone's funeral, I learned from Ange-Marie that Louise was doing very well and that she was in remission from her cancer.

Not surprisingly, before writing these pages, I'd never whispered to anyone about the secret Simone had confided to me.

28

As she had announced, her soul came back to see me a few times to reassure me and confirm that everything was going well for her. She also wanted to leave me a personal message for her great daughter, Anne.

Today, I know that Simone was the one who broke down my doubts and triggered my work with the souls of the dead. Thanks to her, some deep memories of mine came back to me. It was undeniable. I will always feel an infinite gratitude to her for her presence in my life, even though it was disconcerting at the time.

I know that souls who have loved each other even briefly on Earth always keep in contact in infinity. So one day....

Since that time, I have matured, and it seems important to me to return to a point already discussed. Some of the rare beings that we call "Masters of Wisdom" act sometimes like Simone did, like a disciple who can discern the "deeper story."

Simone, herself, was not one of these masters. However, I was able to understand that her decision stemmed from a deep connection with Louise, and her ability to accomplish the exchange had nothing to do with know-how on her part. What happened was simply the result of her awareness of what is now called a "karmic link." No one imagines being able to "take the sickness" of a loved one to escape this world and flee from personal suffering.

As for Ange-Marie, she died about one year after Simone. I'll share more about her soon in a future chapter. For now, I invite you to join me in helping other souls. This is a promise I made.

"A soul always gathers with its own hands, with patience, love, and will, one after another, all flowers that will form one day, the bouquet of its radiance. A being is building himself, in truth, more than he is built. A matter of personal decision because the spark of the Divine expands only where room is made for it. All the room!"[8]

Chapter II

A Black Rose

"You are a circumstance, and I am one too! On the contrary, there is nothing pejorative about it. One circumstance is a decision and a movement of the Divine in his Creation, something sacred and magical that allows new opportunities for flowering."
— *Vu d'en Haut* (Seen from Above) by Daniel Meurois

At the beginning of 1986, I was pregnant with my daughter. I was happy with this pregnancy, and I had my mind full of projects. I already had a little boy, and now I was carrying a girl to add to my joy as a young mother.

My cousin Véronique had been a lawyer. She and her fiancé had bought a beautiful house, and they were planning their wedding for the fall in Old Québec. I gladly helped her with home renovations and wedding preparations.

We often exchanged, with joy and carefreeness, our memories of being "sister-cousins" since early childhood. While we were still small, our families regularly traveled together to the East Coast of the United States. However, each time Véro experienced a choking sensation in the car. It was like a panic attack, and when she'd catch her breath, crying, she would always repeat to her parents, *"I don't want to die in the car!"* I was her vacation roommate, and often at night, she'd hold my hand because, like most children, she was afraid of the dark.

Finally, after all these years, happiness was smiling on my cousin, and the future was promising. She was as resplendent as she was pretty!

Véro liked to paint, and she always kept a painting near her bedside, freely open to our viewing and comments. She loved her colored oils and paintbrushes. But more than anything, she liked to paint what she felt. It was, she told me, to exorcise her fears.

One day, as I passed her easel, what I saw left me perplexed. She had painted a huge black rose!

"But Véro, why a black rose? It's a bit gloomy, right? You are in one of the best moments of your life, and you radiate so much! You explode with beauty!"

She burst out laughing and, with her peculiar, hoarse little voice, answered me: "I felt the need to paint it. I don't know why, but this black rose was imposed on me naturally a week ago in a dream."

"Strange," I said. "Anyway, I don't really like this—not because I don't appreciate your painting art that you master so well, but because this painting gives me shivers. Do you have forebodings?"

"No. It is just a feeling of a day. You are really too sensitive! I recognize it is not a joyful painting, but it doesn't matter. The gloom has gone."

Time went by. We were both caught up in the whirlwind of life, and soon I received her wedding announcement. It was in September, and of course I attended. When I kissed Véronique, she touched my belly, rounded by seven months of pregnancy, and asked me spontaneously, "Are you afraid of delivering?"

She had seen right through me. That was her "thing." She would question me and then let me wonder or worry, unconcerned about my response. "Of course, but I don't have a choice," I said. "You're really teasing and not fun! It is in two months."

But she wasn't listening to me anymore. She was talking to another guest who had been waiting behind me to greet her.

On the twentieth of November, I gave birth, and everything went well. I had a beautiful little girl with abundant hair! The black rose was very far from my thoughts.

My cousin kindly visited me in the hospital. She came in like a cool breeze, as usual. She said a happy "Hello" with a smile. She was wearing her unique look, in black velvet, and she leaned over the head of my daughter and placed a soft kiss on her forehead. Her hair always smelled so good!

"She is really beautiful, this little one!" Véronique said. "She looks like an Italian. For me, I think I will never be a mother. I am not programming my life for this."

"I thought like you," I said. "I hadn't planned anything, but I am so happy to have this beautiful, healthy baby! We cannot know what really awaits us. It seems to me that life gives us surprises and plans for each one of us."

"You think?" She seemed surprised. Her little nose twitched up and down, like she was thinking of something. "Maybe! Listen, I have to go now. I took a break from work just for both of you. I'm running all the time!" She waved her hand. "Oh, I almost forgot. Here, look, I bought her a beautiful lavender-colored wool. It is the same color as her eyes. I guessed she would have strange eyes. Do you like it?"

"I love it."

"See you later."

The end-of-year celebrations arrived, and I of course saw Véronique, always beautiful in her black dress with her brown hair. She had an innate elegance that only, certainly, a nobility from another time could explain.

Natural nobility cannot be acquired. The same goes for good taste. They are like trademarks that follow a soul from life to life, whether rich or poor. My cousin expressed hers beautifully.

"Jo?"[9] she said to me at one point, with anxious eyes.

"Yes?"

"I don't want to die old, ending like a wrinkled apple and a burden for my family. I try, but I cannot think of myself as an old person."

"I think that nobody likes really to become old, Véro, but what can we do? We must inevitably accept aging. And there are beautiful old ladies, right?"

"Look at our mothers and aunts," she added, laughing. "We will be superb and eccentric old ladies, but also rebels. Together. Promise?"

I Would Like to See the Sea

The following year, always busy with my work and rather exhausted, I left Canada for a vacation with my two young children and my spouse. It was early July, and we'd planned fifteen days at the beach on the East Coast of America. Seeing the sea has always done me a lot of good!

When I returned, Véronique called me. I remember it was a Thursday night.

"Hello, cousin! It's me. Did the sea do you good?"

"Oh yeah! We had a great time! You know, it reminded me of our vacations with our parents when we were little. So each time, it is like a kind of pilgrimage."

"Yes, that is true. We were there so often."

There was a strange silence.

"Are you OK, Véro?" I asked.

"Yes, I am, only a little nostalgic suddenly and especially very tired. These days, I listen to 'I Would Like to See the Sea' by Michel Rivard on loop in my car. I wanted to tell you precisely at this moment that I leave this weekend to see it, the sea. *'I would like to see the sea and dance with her to defy death.'*"

My cousin was suddenly singing the song over the phone.

"I love this song, Véro, although the lyrics by themselves are quite sinister. I hope it's not a bad sign. You have vacation days, don't you?

"No, only this weekend and Monday. I just want to breathe a little sea air. You gave me the desire to go."

"It is too short, Véro. The trip is too long. You will not be able to rest. What does your husband think of it?"

"He is not too excited. The beach is not his 'cup of tea.' Like you, he thinks this is too short. But you know me; I want to see the sea. She is calling me! I told him that we could leave on Friday night and then we will be there earlier to enjoy it."

"I know it's useless to try to stop you. You're stubborn like a mule! But be careful. The road in Jackman[10] in Maine and all those local roads are dangerous when it's dark. There was another crash last week."

"Yes, yes, I know. Don't worry. We are both drivers, and we will switch if one of us gets tired. I will call you when I return. Bye-bye!"

Rendezvous

Saturday, my phone rang loudly in the silence of the afternoon. A terrible anxiety suddenly rose in me, as if this ringing was ominous. It was July 18.

"Hello? Hello?"

A woman was weeping, and what she was telling me was so terrible that I hung up, without a word, in shock. I realized that it was my mother who had just spoken to me, but what had she told me exactly? Her hesitant words had been so punctuated by sobs that I was having difficulty grasping everything she'd said.

Some pieces of words echoed in my head: "Véro. Dead. Car accident. This morning in Maine."

"Splinters" of sentences slowly began to make sense. In pain, I collapsed, unable to say a single word to my two young children nearby. They looked at me worriedly.

The Accident

Véronique left "to see the sea," as it had been planned with her husband, around four in the morning to make the most of their short weekend break. The beaches of Maine are about a seven-hour drive from Quebec. The drivers of the car that had been behind Véro and her husband were also from Quebec. They described to me how the accident unfolded.

My cousin was driving happily, sunglasses on, when at the angle of a curve in the serpentine drive lined with lakes that constitutes the famous road of Jackman, a kind of 4x4 car with giant wheels came straight at her, leaving her no chance to avoid it. The "monster on wheels" passed over her car, throwing her husband back on the passenger side under the force of the impact.

As for Véronique, trapped in her safety belt, she found herself stuck behind the wheel. The car was nothing more than a pile of scrap metal.

The young couple who had been following in their car, as well as several other motorists who'd witnessed the accident, immediately called the emergency services, while a former rescuer rushed to offer his help by forcing open first the door on the driver's side.

Véro was not dead but very seriously injured. Weakly, she managed to say a few words: "Get me out of here."

It is known that in such cases you should not move the wounded, but the man who came to help my cousin thought he was doing the right thing and, listening only to his heart, took her out of her tomb.

The young woman from the nearest car held my cousin in her arms, the blood flowing from Véro's ears and throat. Véronique was suffocating. She was dying. As for the young "crazy driver" of the huge 4x4, he was totally unscathed.

An ambulance finally arrived after twenty long and endless minutes of waiting. Its drivers immediately got back on the road at full speed to the city of Skowhegan with the two wounded. But it was too late. Some 900 meters (half a mile) away, the driver turned off the siren. Véro had passed.

Later, we learned that the young couple who'd witnessed everything had been so marked by the tragedy of the scene that they'd returned to Quebec, unable to continue their vacation.

A trial took place with the young American driver of the 4x4. He was the son of a sheriff of a small town in Maine and had been drunk at the time of the accident. He was charged with manslaughter and drunk driving. But it is not the story of this young man that I want to tell you.

Skowhegan

As for Véronique's husband, after a delicate surgery he woke up with several broken ribs, a perforated lung, and a broken leg. The doctor, distressed, told him that his wife was deceased, but he did not believe it because he was certain he had seen Véro standing outside the car during his very brief moments of consciousness at the scene. At his request, and since he was immobilized, the medical staff brought Véro to his room so her body could lie next to him. It was a stupefying spectacle even for the emergency physician.

The doctor, with tears in his eyes, left them alone for an hour to allow the survivor to process what had happened and begin his mourning.

Véro's parents never recovered. Her mother is still alive and remains very affected by this loss, while Véro's brother still remembers it with intense emotion. As for her father, it can be said that he died of grief.

My cousin's body was not returned to Quebec for a fortnight. Then there were the formalities. The funeral was very painful, as you can imagine. Her husband was allowed to leave the hospital to attend, as he did not want to miss the ceremony.

It was not the sea that Véronique was meeting that fateful day. She had not even had time to see it. She had an appointment with death. Unconsciously, she knew it. Her soul had given precursory signs. Everything could have been stopped.

Calling for Help

This evening of July 18, I finally went to see the evidence. Véro was really dead, but I felt she was asking for help, my help. I was in a very bad way.

When night came, I managed to leave my body of flesh to go and join her. I knew that she was probably waiting for me. For the soul that travels, distances do not exist.

In the half-light of the morgue, where my cousin's body had been placed after the accident, a diffuse light appeared to me slowly, emitted by the transparent clarity of a presence.

It was the small figure of Véro standing in front of a metal drawer. Tears ran down her pale cheeks, which were blue from the still-recent trauma. What a shock to see her in such a gloomy place!

"I am scared," she said. "I don't understand, Jo. You see me, don't you? Am I dead? There was a big noise in my head and a pain in my neck. Some sounds came out of my lips, and then nothing else. I was waiting for help next to my car, and then I felt sucked up and stretched out on that cold plate. Tell them all that I was there, that I touched them, and that I lived. They did not see me! They were deaf. Is this death? It's horrible! I worked so hard to study, and—wham!—here I am, mowed down by her! I wanted to live. I wanted it with all my heart! You know it. You do too, Jo. I have so much to do still. Could it be that life stops as stupidly as that? I only wanted to see the sea." She was whispering, still in tears. "This is so cruel. I am upset!"

I was there in front of Véronique, arms dangling, heart broken, and totally unable to answer her with something soothing. So I kept quiet with my arm around her shoulder[11], and we sat together on the floor. I waited for her to calm down.

"Talk to me. Talk to me again, Jo. It warms me up a bit. Tell me not to be afraid," she asked me from behind her big black eyes.

"Yes, you are dead, my dear," I said, "and we all are totally devastated by your car accident. You know, I think there are moments one cannot escape because they are parts of your plan of life. But yet, you see. You feel. You're still alive, only you're alive 'differently.' It's like you're just going to another country, a country not so far away. And I can see you, I can touch you, I can speak to you, whatever the name of the country where you are and wherever you will go."

"But I want to stay here with those I love! I do not want to leave for another place, and I do not want to leave anyone!"

A cold wind blew very hard on us, and Véro dissolved in my arms. I remember feeling that as a refusal to hear me on her part, and I knew I had to respect the rhythm of her soul.

I also knew that she would call on me again, that it could not be otherwise, and that I would come back as long as the acceptance of her new state required it. Experiencing tremors and intense nausea, I came back into my physical body. I felt so helpless! I could still smell my cousin's hair and had the taste of blood in my mouth. I thought, "I should have forbidden her from going to the sea! I should have shared my fears with her. It's all my fault! I will never forgive myself!" This night was one of the worst of my life.

The Second Call

"Jo, Jo, it's me!"

I awoke with a start. Véro was there. She wanted to tell me something. A short time had passed since I'd last seen her.

"Listen, for the last two days after the accident, I stood near my body trying to talk to everyone. I went to see Mum. I do not know how, but I melted into her. You understand? I went through her sleeping body, but I just wanted to snuggle up and comfort her. Is this normal? She felt it, I believe, but she went back to sleep, numbed by her sorrow. But look, here I am like a little bird, and it seems I can fly as I please. Is that death too? Being liberated of our heaviness?"

"Yes, Véro," I said, "you are liberated from the weight of your flesh body, and you are starting to understand your other body, a light body that allows you to go where and how you wish. But, listen to me, you must not stay too long here, near us. You still see your family and life on Earth, right? Do not stagnate. It's important to understand this. You must to go toward the Light. Have you seen it, this Light?"

"Do you speak about the white Light? Yes," she said, "but when it appeared to me, I turned back on my steps. I didn't want to go toward it because it was too strong. A beautiful music was rising in it, I think. Only it seems to me that if I get closer to it, I will lose all desire to see you.

It was the light of a sun that I had never seen before, and it was burning so that I had the impression that I could melt forever. I am not ready, you know."

"Take your time. Go with your rhythm. Do not jostle your desires."

Véronique focused her eyes on mine. Yes, she wanted to complete the loop herself.

"Jo, I saw myself with you in the sea. I saw myself from the inside and outside. It was sweet. I needed to feel the warm sand under my feet to better think about my death."

"Yes, I understand."

"I see everything as an upside-down film that runs in a loop. I can start watching and stop the scenes as I want. I can leave this room and move to another place in complete freedom. I fly and go through all things, even through living beings, except you. I can touch and feel you."

40

"If you feel the need to observe, then do it, but do not linger too long. People you loved are waiting for you in your new life. They are your 'family from Heaven,' and there are guides who will help you."

"Guides? Will they will speak to me like you do? I am too divided, so torn! Not yet!"

Suddenly, there was nothing. Véro had gone back to visit her "past from Earth." I came back to myself but was startled when I heard again the voice of my cousin in the silence of the night. She was crying and kept repeating, "I can't! I can't!"

Almost immediately, I felt pulled, and soon I was attached by the mouth to the stained glass window of a church. It was the Saint-Charles Church, from our early childhood and Bible studies. Véro was there, and like me, her mouth was stuck to the stained glass, her white dress unfurled, her eyes completely distraught.

"I cannot talk to them," she said through the stained glass. "They don't see me."

I still remember this scene today with horror and pain. How difficult it is sometimes to help a soul in distress, especially when she is dear to your heart. I would really like to go back and change all the facts that led me here, but there is no way to do this.

A Walker must hide his or her own feelings in order to help. He must ideally keep all his strength to help the suffering soul. Only after will he be able to give himself the time to grieve. Supporting a soul that refuses to pass to the Other Side of the Veil is extremely exhausting, and you must keep a certain distance to avoid being swallowed up by anger, an inevitable sorrow, and an eventual bitterness.

So, while telepathically asking Véronique to follow me, I instinctively breathed very strongly toward her mouth through the stained glass window. It was a white breath. We then went to the scene of her accident—that is to say, in the "memory bubble" that my cousin had created around the carcass of her car. We were both standing there, silent witnesses, watching the repetitive loop of the moment when Véro got out of her car and lost consciousness in the arms of the young woman who had been following her on the road.

We had returned a few days earlier as well, in the early morning. A mist surrounded the scene, a veil behind which there was no hope of escape, no breach. The "bubble" was opaque, gray, and dense.

"So it is true," whispered my cousin in a tired voice. "I am dead."

"Yes," I said. "You've been dead because of this accident for four days now. Remember? Your neck was broken upon impact, and you had severe internal bleeding. Your body is at Skowhegan Hospital. We are waiting for your husband to be ready to take the ambulance with you for your funeral."

The details of her death no longer seemed to interest her.

"Jo, where is the white Light? I don't see it. She disappeared forever? Am I condemned to stay here like a ghost that no one sees or hears except for you? I do not want to be a prisoner of a car carcass! I want to leave this road!"

"You are still alive, Véro. I will repeat it to you. You just vibrate differently. You vibrate in another frequency, and the body of your soul is no longer held in your flesh. You are in your luminous copy, perfectly intact and healing from the wounds of your car accident. The Light will come back as soon as you integrate the acceptation of your death. Entities—"

"How? Entities?"

"'Guides of the Light,' if you like that better. They will come back again to invite you to your new life and to find your family up above."

"In Paradise? In Heaven?"

"No. Yes, if you want. We call it the Astral world. This is your new home, your new country. You will know it when you cross its threshold. Look, there is a blue ray that is beginning to emerge and will dissolve this mist around us. They are the ones. Are you ready? They heard your opening. The guides come to you. Do you see them?"

"Yes, I see this Light again. It is so warm, so comforting, and I am so cold here. Tell me, if I cross now, will I be able to see you again? I still have things to do, to say...."

"Yes, you will see. At the beginning, you will come back often, but after a while, you will detach yourself from your painful memories because you will have started a new life."

Véronique then didn't listen to me anymore, fascinated by what she was starting to see.

There was a kind of pale blue explosion, then only blue light. The accident scene disappeared. I smiled and saw Véronique walk toward the Presences of Light, without turning around once.

Then there was nothing. I found myself alone, recalled to my body lying on my bed.

The White Dress of Véro

Three weeks had passed since the tragedy. She was so beautiful at the funeral, my cousin, in her white silk dress, with her hair around her face. A bouquet of roses and white lilies, from me, had been placed against her heart. The flowers caressed the blue mark left by the safety belt that had broken her neck. She was wearing an immaculate dress and freshwater pearls. It was really the best, it seemed to me, so she could go to her final rendezvous.

As I approached, I smoothed one of her hair strands to set it according to her habit, and then I kissed her wrinkle-free forehead, which was cold and hard as marble.

The Goodbye

The time had finally come. The funeral procession for Véro wandered under the hot sun of August. Her coffin of white

43

wood, covered with beautiful roses and ferns, exploded with light and contrasted with all the people dressed in black who followed it.

I walked with them also, of course, head down in my black dress, silent and sad at the beginning of the group, with the relatives.

We were missing Véronique so much. She had such great joy! A pure diamond. Suddenly, a strong breeze blew, lifting my hair and forcing me to raise my head. I was almost annoyed. It was like an intruder, this wind that had interrupted the flow of my thoughts.

That's when I saw my cousin. She was standing next to our solemn parade, which suddenly seemed strange to me. She was looking at me intensely. Then with her hand, she twisted off one of the white roses from her coffin so that it came to me. Taken aback, I received it against my chest.

No one else seemed to see her.

But Véro was there, airy, beautiful as an angel. She smiled at me, and with her hand, she blew me a kiss.

The message was received. My cousin told me that everything was fine. We parted at this precise moment with a tender embrace of our souls. I will never forget the intensity of this caress. She then disappeared, and the white rose intoxicated me.

The black rose had belonged to her "past on Earth," such a short passage without a hiccup.

A "goodbye" is never a farewell. It is a living promise! I indeed saw my cousin Véronique on the Other Side of the Veil, frequently and for several helps to the Passage.

What You Need to Know about Accidental Deaths

A fatal accident creates a huge state of shock for a soul expelled from his or her body very brutally. Immediately after the impact and death, the soul must realize that she no longer has a body of flesh and no longer belongs to the earth plane. Most of the time, such a brutal disembodiment distorts the perception of reality between the two worlds. Since accident victims still believe they are alive because they have not been through the Passage process, their souls struggle to see the help of the guides around them. They are thus often frozen between two vibratory spaces and confused.

The soul may be panicked because they had not considered or seen death coming, like someone who had a long illness, for instance. We must be very caring and loving with such a soul in order to explain to them, in simple terms, what happened and to help them integrate the transition to the other vibratory planes that await them.

It is important to understand the momentary fragility of this soul and to treat them with delicacy and great respect for their body. If you witness an accident in which a person dies, you can start internally explaining to him or her the nature of what happened and reassuring them while protecting their physical body from the eyes of the curious. This will enable the guides and walkers to carry out their supporting job more easily.

Chapter III

Emma's Story

"You understand that we are all bound by contracts—fathers-mothers, parents-children, directors-workers, rulers-citizens, and murderers-murder victims—without forgetting that these contracts only mention links in a very limited sense, since in one life you are, for example, father, son, prince, husband, president, and Christian, and that each of these positions creates multiple contracts with the entourage."

— *Le voyage vers les sphères célestes
(Journey to the Celestial Spheres)* by Johanne Razanamahay

Emma was living with her mother in a nice part of Massachusetts, in the United States. Her house made of gray cedar shingles, with its pretty shutters and large white wood porch, was close to the sea. Wild roses bloomed near the door, and the home was framed at the back by large conifers. It was a fragrant place, scented by the pines and the salty smell of the Atlantic Ocean a few hundred feet away.

Emma rarely saw her father. Her conception had been an "accident" resulting from her mother and father's brief fling. Her father did not even come to the maternity ward when she was born.

Having a child would encroach on his freedom too much, he said shortly after her birth. Despite acknowledging his paternity, he certainly didn't want to support the child. It was not his plan for the future, he repeated to Louise, Emma's mother and one of our close friends. Fortunately, she was very well organized. It was more difficult to tolerate him than to raise his daughter alone.

Life had been peaceful throughout Emma's childhood because Louise worked as a pharmacist in Quebec and had enough savings to be the sole breadwinner. Emma's father was a pharmaceutical representative.

When Louise received a more lucrative job offer in the United States, Emma's father was, at the time, on sick leave for depression. Even though he really hadn't ever been concerned about his daughter, he was not happy that she was leaving Canada. After obtaining a residence permit, Louise moved to start her new job in Boston and found a new house near the ocean. She immediately set up a pretty room for her daughter. Emma had expressed specific design ideas and adored the sea air.

The young teenager also loved animals. She had a big cat that followed her everywhere. Her dream was to become a veterinarian. When she told us about it, her eyes sparkled. Then, one day, fate suddenly intervened.

A Clinic

Sitting in a medical office, Louise was in tears. Her doctor had just confirmed what she'd feared for a few months: a diagnosis of advanced cancer of the uterus. It was a blow to a mother worried about the future of her daughter. Louise put on a brave face, but "her cancer," as she called it, obviously caused her despair.

Although the atmosphere of the house was not ideal for the mother and daughter, both felt hopeful for better days ahead. Louise and Emma continued to live as "normally" as possible in spite of the severity of Louise's disease.

Alas, the cancer evolved quickly, and despite aggressive chemo treatments, a vegetarian and "hyperorganic" diet, energy-related therapies, and even visits to some healers, Louise was soon declared incurable and transferred to palliative care.

However, she did not want to be hospitalized "to the end" but rather wanted to spend her last days in her pine-scented house, wrapped in the ocean air she loved so much and surrounded by her friends and relatives. Everyone began taking turns at her side, night and day. She even had a special room to facilitate the nursing care she received. Louise was loved and well-cared-for. There was an improvised mattress on the floor of the living room for her companions, right next to the imposing stone fireplace, so they could hear Louise when she called.

It was December, and the cold was felt on the Atlantic coast.

Reconnection

Then began a long agony, an extreme suffering that went on and on. Feeling exhausted and her end nearing, Louise asked to see Emma's father again. (I will call him "John" here.) Worried about her daughter, she wanted to talk to him soon. John made the trip and came to see her at home. Only Louise and John were in the room when they met, so there were no witnesses to what was really said and then signed. It was John who later gave his version to relatives and friends. Some learned directly from her that she had given him a significant amount of money in cash for her funeral and he was to then also provide for their daughter. She'd also agreed that he could rent her house until Emma was old enough to inherit it.

He had the notary papers in his hand then, naming him the guardian of his daughter and all her property. John had apparently reassured Louise by promising to look after Emma until she came of age. There was no way Louise could have known the immense mistake she'd made in putting her daughter's destiny in the hands of such a man. A few months later, Louise died in the presence of her family and friends. I was there with my husband. It was a few days before Christmas, December 20, at seven in the morning.

Placing the Casket in the Ground

I can still see Emma with her long auburn hair at the burial, dignified in her navy coat, her big blue scarf wrapped around her graceful neck. She was dazed by grief and fear. In front of all those present, she threw the first white rose onto her mother's coffin.

I was there, not far away, and one thing made me feel uncomfortable: Her father was obviously saving a lot based on the type of coffin that had been selected to hold the lean body of Emma's mother. He was there, with all the friends and relatives, trying to make a good impression on Louise's family. They watched him with suspicion. And then there was Emma, a little orphan of fourteen, obliged to live with this man, almost a stranger. It was hard.

Emma's whole body trembled. She was in shock. What would become of her? I am sure that everyone who attended Louise's funeral was thinking the same as me, all of us.

Life had not given her any other choice. No one could take care of her without John's consent.

Faced with this opportunity and seeing the money in his bank account, John suddenly felt a swell of paternal feeling and perfectly fit to take care of his daughter. His once-reclaimed freedom was now a thing of the past, that of a crazy youth. His daughter suddenly became really important to him—his only family.

After the funeral, John moved Emma into his home in Cape Cod. He had recently left his job in Canada and decided to put everything into living in the United States. Having dual citizenship because of his father, it was easy for him. The house, inside and out, was a mess, like a cottage in a wasteland. He said he had recently bought it for very little money to get closer to Louise and Emma. He had, he said, plans for renovation, but it was apparent he was comfortable with his semi-slum.

As for Emma, she struggled with her new circumstances but had to make do, though she greatly missed her mother's house and her beautiful childhood bedroom. She'd brought her cat with her, but he ran away from this gloomy place and never came back again. Cats are very sensitive, and a human aura never lies to them. That of Emma's father had obviously not pleased him. The young teenager therefore continued her studies under these circumstances, although very depressed by the loss of her mother. Françoise, her grandmother, bought her another purebred cat, a Maine Coon, one of those so-called giant cats from this area of the East Coast of the United States. She hoped the cat would make Emma smile and keep her company. Françoise felt so helpless in the face of all this, unable to recover from the death of her daughter.

Fortunately, Emma quickly became attached to her cat and gave him a lot of attention and love. He was beautiful! He was her confidante. She adored him and wanted to one day breed the cat, with John's consent, before beginning her veterinary studies.

My husband and I had been very close friends with Louise when she lived in Quebec with Emma. That's why we continued to visit Emma regularly in the United States.

And it's why we also tried many times after Louise's death to invite Emma to our home. We even offered to care for her to give her a more comfortable life than the one John was imposing on her.

We were very affected by this situation and shared many of our concerns with her grandmother. Unfortunately, Emma's father had decision-making authority because she was a minor. His answer to our invitations was always the same: "No!"

We could not even get her to come for a short visit or a few vacation days during the summer. John, in the meantime, had lost his job due to serious alcohol problems.

A while after Louise's funeral, the notary responsible for the case telephoned the family to inform them that John had not yet paid for the funeral services. The picture was now complete.

The notary claimed that John received only a small income from unemployment and that his bank account was very low. We were astonished, and the notary was told that John had informed several people that Louise's savings had been given to him before she died, as well as very precise instructions for her burial. According to the notary, John was not taking care of Emma very well. In small, rural communities, everyone knows everything. Obviously, the large sum of money that Louise had entrusted to John for her funeral had been used for something other than what it was intended for. It was very clear how it should have been spent, as Louise had also spoken about it to me directly several months before her death. So where did Louise's money go?

After some digging, it was discovered that John had squandered the funds unscrupulously and bought a big Hummer truck. Many had seen it at Louise's house. He preferred to let himself live, surviving on Louise's savings and renting Emma's house while keeping her relatives, cousins, and friends away from her. Sometimes, he allowed Emma to go spend a few days with her cat at an older cousin's country house. This allowed him to receive some women at his home and go to the village port for drinks.

According to what we heard, John became violent when he drank, and Emma was careful not to confront him. She "bought" her peace and prepared all his meals so as to not make waves. As for Louise's house, it was rented by unsavory people, perfect strangers, people John met on random nights of drinking. He couldn't get the rental money from the tenants because he was afraid of them. His daughter was obviously not informed of all this. All the while, Emma was growing up and approaching the age of majority. How eager she was to gain her independence, to take back her house and finally be free of her father's weight! Yet Emma was far from aware of all his misdeeds.

On the morning of December 31, when he told her he had to repair some damage caused by the recent tenants before they'd fled without paying the rent, she asked to go with him to make an assessment of the place and see what there was to do before returning to her "home."

She was so excited! In a month and a few days, the transfer of the inheritance would finally take place. She would henceforth be free to continue her relations with her father or live without his presence. She had taken driving lessons and amassed a small amount of money to buy a used car. She hoped to rent one of the rooms to a good friend in college.

"Can I come, Dad?" Emma asked. "I will help you with the cleaning and painting. I know how. I'm good at working with my hands."

After a long hesitation, John accepted.

"Well, I'll warn you: There are lots of things to arrange," he said.

Emma donned a dark blue jumpsuit and tied her long auburn hair behind her head under a matching cap. She was tall, and from a distance, she could easily have been mistaken for a worker.

She had time. She had already prepared everything for the New Year's Eve party that very evening. Her older cousin, her arms loaded with gifts, had made the trip early in the morning to bring her some pastries and a good bottle of champagne. Emma had done odd jobs during the holidays and saved for this moment. "In a month," she had announced with obvious pride, "I will recover my house, and I will move in with my two cats and a friend. I will do breeding. The land is big enough."

On the Way

In the early afternoon, during the drive to her childhood home where she had grown up with her mother, Emma quickly noticed how much her father already smelled of alcohol. He was nervous and obviously on the defensive.

Arriving at the house, she burst into tears upon seeing the extent of the damage done to the property and the grounds. John had hidden many things from her and certainly also lied.

Stray and wild animals had lived inside the house. The living room, kitchen, and even the floor had all been ransacked. The antique wood furniture had been chewed on. Everything smelled. The interior would have to be redone completely. As for the outside, the shutters had been thrown to the ground among the detritus and the garden. And as for the garden, farewell to the roses and fine herbs! Even the beautiful pines had been cut down to build a dog pen. The land was nothing more than waste and mud. The large wooden deck was totally faded.

Seeing the reaction of his daughter and fearing that the neighbors could hear, John said to her, "I told you. Don't worry. I can fix it with some friends. Twelve thousand, and it will just have been a bad dream. You'll be able to move in by February as expected."

"God! You have to hear yourself! Twelve thousand dollars?" Emma yelled. "Where are you going to get that? How could you have let it deteriorate to such a point, and without warning me? It was not you! You certainly haven't come by to see it often. It was not you! As usual, you were closing your eyes, preferring to drink at the town pub. You drank away my inheritance without guilt, Dad! This was what Mom left me. I don't have the words to describe what you did to Mom and me!"

"Don't scream so loud," John said, his lips tightening as he pushed her to a more discreet corner of the house. "Someone will hear you, and the neighbors will come back."

"I can finally tell you what I think of you! I wanted to have a joyful celebration with you, in peace, tomorrow evening. I am really stupid!"

First of the Year

The telephone rang loudly in our room. We both took a quick look at the alarm. Who would be calling on the first of the year at seven o'clock in the morning? It was surely important.

Our hearts were tight. My spouse picked up the phone and put it on speakerphone.

"Hello?" he said.

The call was from the United States. The voice of Kate, one of Louise's best friends, was trembling and hesitant. Then, finally, Kate said in a single cry mixed with sobs, "A terrible misfortune has happened to Emma!"

"Oh no! What happened? She had an accident?"

"She committed suicide yesterday afternoon."

"But, this is impossible. She was in good spirits. We just talked to her two days ago! She had just gotten another cat, and she was a month away from her majority, with all that it meant!"

"I don't know more. They refuse to give me more details, and her father remains silent."

"Do you have his cell phone number? We are calling him. After all, Louise was one of our best friends, and he knows very well how we handled her funeral."

I turned on the light, and we went upstairs to try to find John's number in our files. After finding it and dialing, we finally heard (again through speakerphone) a "Hello" pronounced by a male voice. He sounded very confused, monotonous, presumably under the influence of a substance.

"John, is it you? What happened at home?" I asked. "Kate just called to tell us that Emma is deceased. A suicide! This is impossible! Tell us this is a bad dream!"

"Yes, she committed suicide. I found her when I returned home yesterday night around 7:00 p.m. I'm sorry. I'm in shock."

"Where? How? What are you talking about?"

"In the garden. She hanged herself. I quickly cut the rope, but it was too late. I called the police, and they declared her dead, unfortunately."

"But Louise's cousin told us she saw her preparing for New Year's Eve and cleaning the house. Why would she hang herself? And after the purchase of her second cat? It's impossible to believe!"

"I don't know how to explain her actions. She was already very depressed and suicidal after the death of her mother, and well, you know. Fortunately, back then, we were able to save her."

"What? You're trying to explain her act with this old story? That was a long time ago."

In the space of a moment, I remembered Emma's suicide attempt. She was only fourteen, and I had often wondered why her father had never brought Louise's powerful painkillers back to the pharmacy after her death, as it was logical to do so. Emma had taken them.

"I did my best to make things nice for her," John said, stammering but emphatic. "Since then, I made her a little closed room and a private toilet. You did not see."

I was stunned. I knew his way of turning things to his advantage.

"The sheriff took her to the morgue. The police summoned the coroner, but he could only deduce death by hanging," John added.

"And you? Where were you? Emma told us that you were often absent."

"I had gone to do some work at Louise's house. Emma was to inherit it in a month. The tenants had neglected the house. So I was doing some painting with a friend. I didn't want to worry Emma with these problems. I wanted to move a little faster. Emma called me around three o'clock in the afternoon to tell me that she was waiting for me for supper. When I returned, I found her."

A painful silence then settled between us.

"We'll take the first plane out to assist the family with the funeral arrangements for Emma," I finally said. "We absolutely want to see her again and the places, if possible. Louise,

56

Emma, and us—we were very close despite the impediments. You know it. Wait until we get there to decide on the date of the funeral."

It was January 1 and a weekend. It was difficult to find a flight. During the holidays, most flights are fully booked.

"You won't be able to see the place because the sheriff sealed it off as a crime scene," John said. "This is normal while awaiting the continuation of the investigation and the final report of the coroner. A full autopsy will take about a week. The police said that the scene spoke for itself. I will wait for you. I will call you back when I have more details. But on your side, with your abilities, can I ask you something?"

"What do you mean?"

"Uh, if Emma ever gets in touch with you, like about where she is, or if she tries to explain her actions, you will tell me, right? I would like to know."

"We will try to see. But it's Emma's choice to make the move if she wants. We must avoid soliciting those who leave. By the way, what did you do with the cats?"

"They are at my girlfriend's place, and I am living there too."

John hung up, and we got ready for an emergency departure. We called him back that evening to tell him that we'd found a flight for January 3 to New York and would be arriving soon. John then told us that it would be too late, because the burial had been scheduled for the morning of January 3 at 10:00 a.m. He said that the coroner had determined her death to be a suicide, and, given her depressive history, there would be no autopsy. Also, it was the holidays. Everyone, including the doctors and police, was eager to celebrate the New Year, and that was understandable. They had their families to be concerned about.

"Why don't you wait for us? What does it matter to wait for us? Why so much rush to bury Emma? Is it that you do not want us to see her?" I asked him.

John seemed to be embarrassed more than really affected.

57

"Oh, I like doing things faster," he said. "Her body will not be embalmed, because of Louise and Emma's beliefs, and I can't wait to be done with these painful images. She will be briefly on view tomorrow at a wake, the evening of January 2, and then again the morning of January 3, followed by burial immediately after that."

"But John, Emma had a violent death, and you are rushing to bury her like this without any ceremony. Why are you doing this?"

We did not know what to say anymore. Something was wrong with all of this.

"I am taking sedatives. I'm exhausted! This family is bad luck," he exclaimed finally before hanging up on us.

First Contact

We canceled our flight. On January 3, very early in the morning, I went into meditation to try to help Emma remotely without entering her own world. It was the expected time of her funeral.

Suddenly, I felt a kind of cold corridor next to me. It was Emma. My eyelids closed, I saw her running in another "vibratory channel" parallel to the room I was in. It was like a foggy and gloomy tunnel.

It's a difficult perception to explain. The room I was meditating in seemed to be in color, while the other was in black and white and separated from mine by a thread. I kept seeing Emma running in all directions, in a state of panic. I could see her jeans and belt very well, but there were some kinds of parasites on our line of communication. The image was cut off, and then her face reappeared to me, frightened. All of this was terrible, and it looked like a request for help.

"Emma, is that you? I see you," I said. "Calm down. I am going to try to help you. Can you talk to me?"

"Yes, Marie." I heard her very weakly before the image of her presence disappeared totally.

58

Invaded by a feeling of acute anguish, I began to pray for Emma. Mantra after mantra, accompanied by a candle flickering, I said a string of prayers. Finally, I told my husband what I had seen and heard. Like me, he understood that there was a lot of work to do and help to provide. First, we decided to leave our bodies to join Emma and comfort her with our presence and support.

An uncommon scene awaited us at the cemetery. As expected, the ceremony had just ended, and the people present were near Emma's father, who was quiet. They were offering their condolences to him. Not far from there, Emma's form of light was waiting in her father's big blue sport utility vehicle. She had her head resting against the window, and her runaway cat was with her. She had brought him into her "energy airlock."[12]

"Emma," I told her, "understand us well. We are with you. I know you can hear us. Come back to see us when you are ready to talk more."

Emma looked at us with empty eyes and told us, "Are they burying me right now? I am here. I am alive. I can feel and see them. Tell them and *him*."

"'Him' who? Your father? Emma, listen, you are dead to this Earth. This is true. But as you can see, this death is not the reality. Your life goes on. You are talking and hearing us."

Emma was crying with her head down. She stopped speaking and said no more.

My husband and I then came back into our physical bodies very affected and full of questions about what Emma had meant by emphasizing "him." Obviously, she felt very bad and was trying to make us understand something.

Second Contact

We were finishing dinner one night when, all of a sudden, I closed my eyes. Emma was sitting on the chair next to me, facing my husband. He quickly realized that she wanted to talk to me without his presence as a male, out of shyness. He left the room, giving me time to be alone with her.

A telepathic communication was immediately established between Emma and me for a good thirty minutes. She showed me different scenes in pictures, and it was like seeing the sequences of a movie inside her. I then began to comment on them to check with her as to whether I understood their meaning. I described to her what I perceived, and she nodded when a comment was correct.

An immense sadness emanated from Emma, and today I still feel it—a great cold that freezes my hands and hurts my heart. I had so strongly felt what she'd experienced—her pain and the fear within her.

"Emma, are you ready to tell me about the afternoon of December 31? I mean, what really happened."

"Yes, I want to reveal all. Mum is with me. She told me that you will help me, and your husband, Daniel, will too."

"I will do my best. You can count on me, on us, Emma. Send me images, but not all at the same time because I have difficulty placing them in order." Emma briefly nodded her head and communicated other scenes, more slowly this time.

With my eyes closed, I saw her get out of a vehicle with her father. She was wearing a long, one-piece, navy cotton jumpsuit. I recognized it because it was what she usually wore to do outdoor painting work. John was there, and they had a very heated discussion.

Then I saw detailed pictures of Louise's house. The images appeared to me one after another. Some of the beautiful furniture Louise had bought from an antiques dealer in Cape Cod was scattered outside. Emma's pretty white wrought-iron bed was covered in mud and animal excrement. There were shards of glass lying around from shattered windows, and broken shutters littered the ground, as well as dead rose bushes. The property had become a garbage dump, and the house had been damaged. The scene made me sick.

"Oh no, Emma! Is this what you discovered when you went to see the house on December 31?"

"Yes!" she shouted in a sob. "He lied to me. All my life, he lied to me. He used me."

"That's why you made this fatal decision? You ended your life for this, my little Emma? We would have helped you to remodel your house with your cousins and friends."

Emma cried again before vanishing. Then there was nothing. Emma had gone back to her psychic lock. Deep inside, I knew that she would come back. I also knew that her reaction was logical because her soul was scattered and completely exhausted. She needed to make her way slowly, to get rid of the unspeakable.

I told my husband about all the scenes Emma had shown me. We understood that the sight of her vandalized home had turned her upside down.

How could one be insensitive to what she had lived through at that moment, a few months from finally being able to reclaim her mother's house? This place that was once so pretty, where the pine groves and the ocean charmed us so much. How? Did her indignation explain her suicide? Even though the house would need work, does one commit suicide after preparing for a New Year's Eve party and buying a new, beloved pet? Emma had become so strong, so brave. She was no longer the fourteen-year-old little girl struggling under the weight of losing her mother.

Repeated Calls

While Emma was "telling us" about her tragedy in small, hesitating bits, John was trying to find out what she was saying. He called us all the time, flooding our answering machine with his questions. Rather than crushed by the pain, he was in a total panic. We didn't respond to him, despite the cruelty of the situation. Something told us that we needed to know first and foremost what had *really* happened.

We had friends who lived near Louise's house. I had the idea to ask them to take pictures of the damage the property had suffered. It did not take long. As soon as I received the pictures on my computer, I compared them to the "pictorial sequences" I'd perceived during my contacts with Emma.

Why, I wondered, in her successive contacts did Emma always show me the same "pictures" of an outside corner of her mother's house?

I could see an angle of the house a little sheltered from the neighborhood and a garden hose rolled out. Why did she show me this? As some kind of evidence? She probably wanted me to discover something. Proof? But proof of what exactly? If she did really commit suicide, what was she trying to make me understand by showing me this hose and this corner of the house?

The key to the story was probably in one of the photos from my friends, and with Emma's help, we absolutely had to discover it not only for ourselves but also to open for her the subtle doors leading to her real "light house."

Third Contact

A hand gently brushed against my face in the darkness of the night. She insisted on getting me out of my sleep. I jumped. It was Emma's hand.

"Is that you, my sweetheart? Are you here to show me something? I didn't understand everything, but we will get there together. I asked your mother's friends to take pictures of your house."

"I know. But you don't understand everything. You cannot see what I want you to see. Come with me. Come. I want to show you."

It was almost instantaneous. I was already moving to Emma's side with my Body of Light. We were at her place, at a place called Pine Point. Emma had a closed expression on her face and remained very quiet. How tall she seemed!

"Are you angry at me, Emma?"

"I am angry at *him* because I am in so much pain, too much pain. I wanted to live! Do you understand? If only you knew how unfair this is!"

"Him? So you *did* want to live? What are you trying to tell me?" I looked for her eyes. "This is not where you wanted to end up, right? Tell me."

Emma looked at me fixedly, for a long time, and I knew her answer.

"You didn't commit suicide, did you? You were murdered!"

"*Here*," she said, showing me with her hand the side of the house where the garden hose was.

I walked to this dark corner. It formed an angle with the extension that housed a small pavilion for friends. The garden hose was still there, running toward us. Emma immediately showed me her neck. It still bore the blue traces of the hose.

"That's how he choked me," she said painfully. "It wasn't me. It was him! The truth must be revealed! He took me to his house in his car, and then he placed me under the big pine with a rope around my neck. It was not me! Not me. I had a lot of projects. I wanted to live."

Emma disappeared suddenly, and I returned to my body, where it had been lying.

The next day, still very disturbed by what Emma had tried to make me hear, I reopened the files of the photos that friends of Louise had sent me, and I feverishly looked for one photo showing the outside of the house. "Yes, here he is!" I said to myself. The garden hose was on the lawn just as Emma had shown me, meaning she had died there.

Had John lied this much, telling the police that he'd found her hanged at his house around 7:00 p.m. in the garden? We still lacked answers, and only Emma could give them.

Fourth Contact

Sitting in the living room, I quickly felt the presence of Emma at my side. She was not alone. On the other armchair, I recognized her mother, our friend Louise. Her countenance seemed tortured and tense, like she was suffering.

"Louise, you came as well?" I asked.

"Yes," she said to me with a brief nod. "I want you to understand the facts so that Emma does not bear, in the eyes of all, the stigma of an act she did not commit! Everything is my fault. I should never have trusted him! If only you knew my regret!"

"You are talking about Emma's father, right?"

"Yes, *him*! She did not commit suicide. John staged it so as not to be accused of the murder of his own daughter. He probably did not want to kill her, but his violence caught up with him."

"I will avenge myself," Emma exclaimed in her psychic prison. "He took my life away from me when I had so many projects."

They then both left our living room. Soon, I felt great stomach pains, and a terrible weight pressed on my heart. The idea of revenge has always chained a soul to Earth. But it would be impossible to leave things like this! I told my husband everything, and he was totally stunned by the revelations of Louise and Emma. Though I'd never liked Emma's father, discovering what he had done was still a shock for me. How could he live with this act in his conscience?

Fifth Contact

At my request, Daniel went out of his body with me to meet Emma. I did not want to be wrong. Quickly, our subtle bodies were directly next to the yellow garden hose. Emma was there already. She was waiting for us.

"Tell us, Emma," Daniel said, "did Marie Johanne understand correctly what you revealed to her? Did she fully understand?"

"Some parts, but not all. She doesn't want to understand it all."

"Is it about this garden hose, Emma? This one that you constantly show her?"

"Yes."

"This is where you died? Not at your father's place, under the big pine tree?"

"Yes. I thought I was clear. He became nervous because I was upset, and he was drunk. I was screaming too loudly. He grabbed me and wrapped the garden hose around my neck to try to quiet me down. I fainted, and everything went black. It was an accident. He carried my inanimate body to his truck and then tied me to a rope, to suggest something else. Then he alerted the police. He panicked because of what he had done. He didn't think I was going to die, but see my neck? These are not the traces of a rope but of a garden hose."

Emma closed her eyes.

She eventually snuggled into our open arms, relieved of her burden. She was not ready to join the Light yet, though, because she was still talking about revenge.

In the following days, we contacted the sheriff and the lawyer-doctor who'd hastily concluded that Emma's death was a suicide.

We shared our doubts and included many testimonials from friends of the family, including the cousin who'd seen Emma just before her death and a neighbor who'd noticed John on December 31 in the company of a "worker" dressed in a suit and cap.

We also forwarded emails that Emma had sent us that proved she had projects going on and was happy. As far as our contacts with Emma and her mother and the precise and truthful recollection of the events, it was impossible to discuss this with the authorities, as it would have had no credibility in their eyes. We completed application forms for questioning the investigation as well as asking for an exhumation of the body if possible, hoping an autopsy would reveal the true cause of death. Much time went by before we even got a response from the sheriff. He stated flatly that it was too late to reopen the investigation because the body had not been embalmed.

We were furious and felt so helpless in the face of this enormous tragedy. Emma, encamped in her anger, often came to visit us in her own way. One evening, in front of her, I sent a text message to her father, who had not stopped harassing us to find out if Emma had spoken.

I remember writing to him, "Yes, John, Emma has spoken to us. We have heard about what happened. We know what you did to your daughter. Do not contact us anymore. May you be able to live with that."

After receiving this message, John stopped all attempts to contact us, not even to try to convince us of the opposite. It was a form of confession. He probably felt unable to plead his innocence.

John finally disappeared from the small seaport of Cape Cod, probably seeking to be forgotten and erase the drama of his conscience. We never saw him again. Only a few people crossed paths with him.

But things did not stop there. Emma had freed herself from her story, but her soul was not at peace and did not leave Earth. She wandered as if she wanted to settle in our home until her father was accused of murder.

I worked with her for over two months, trying to teach her to erase her wounds and anger piece by piece. It was necessary to discuss this with her, to bring her some peace. I told her that it was too late to go back, that anger and hate were making prison bars that were invisible but real, and that the Beings of Light were waiting for her to pursue another life, a life elsewhere.

One evening, when she was standing between two worlds near me, she finally exclaimed with a smile, the very first since her death, "Marie, I see them! They are here, these beings that you described to me. And I also see my grandmother, grandpa, and mum... and my old cat. Oh, the house and the garden too!"

"You see, my sweetheart, I told you life goes on. Your home sweet home is ready to welcome you again. Go! Join them. Go rest now. You are always alive! You have just changed vibrations, like changing a TV channel. From now on, you can create whatever you want, do what you love, rebuild your ideal."

I saw Emma turn to her mother and grandmother and then reach for her cat before heading to her own world, the one that perfectly matched the color of her soul.

Surprise

A few months passed, and then the big figure of Emma again appeared before me. Her beautiful face was relaxed. It reflected a lovely blue light, and her eyes shone like two sapphires. Emma was rejuvenated, it seemed to me, or maybe that was the effect her soul wanted to offer me at that precise moment.

"Marie, thank you," she said. "Tell the ones I love that I am doing well and have found other paths, other souls with experiences like I had. Together, we evolve, we heal, and we are at peace. It will be necessary for John to heal too. I don't really blame him anymore. I even have several cats now. Look at how cute they are!" She had a big smile on her face.

As she said that, I saw a family of little Maine Coons coming happily to meet her. This vision, this message that Emma had just given me, made me feel good in my heart.

Emma's soul, however, came back to see me later. You will learn more in another story in this book.

About Murder Victims

A murdered person, just like the victim of an accident, has the impression that they left too early, that they were pulled out of life before "their time."

By taking stock of life in the momentary space of wandering, the Kamaloca, this soul has the opportunity to refine him- or herself, to go beyond fears and resentments to reach the famous "paradise," the Devachan that is unique to each individual. They will find other souls there wishing to return quickly to Earth and thus heal from past wounds.

In cases similar to Emma's, the soul will often reincarnate into his or her immediate family or with other relatives to reconnect and work on what was left unresolved.

Hasty returns are frequent. Yet it is crucial for a soul to take the time to heal in his own Kamaloca and then join his Devachan before considering a return to Earth. An earthly return too fast sometimes repeats an unhealthy pattern.

According to my own observations, the moment of departure seems fixed for each one of us. What is written in one's "contract of incarnation" is always done at the "right time," that of the Divine Plan traced in a soul in spite of the circumstances, sometimes difficult, of her death.

This may seem cruel to those who remain after a departure in tragic circumstances, but in the large wheel of incarnations, there is always a reason for that, a teaching. Any event is an opportunity to grow.

Chapter IV

Cindy

"Imagination is always the strongest! She's the one who runs the man wherever he goes. So in the first moments after death, the soul of the deceased enters the world she expected to find. If the deceased is an atheist during his terrestrial life, he will remain, as long as the light will be in his mind, in a kind of black porridge, indefinable, necessarily unpleasant, which he thought he would find after death."

— *Récits d'un Voyageur de l'Astral (Stories of a Traveler of the Astral Realm)* by Daniel Meurois and Anne Givaudan

It was a weekday morning like any other. There was nothing to suggest what was going to happen, not yet at least.

Cindy, a young woman in her thirties, was already late for work. She had a busy day waiting for her at the Salon de Coiffure, where she was employed. She was driving fast on a small departmental road in the Toulouse area in France.

She was immersed in her thoughts, and the last words she'd exchanged with her husband were still ringing in her head. When she left, she'd slammed the door of the house they had just built for their family. He did not understand anything!

"He does not know," she murmured to herself, "how furious I am to live in myself, how much more than ever I feel a sense of urgency, as if tomorrow were not certain. There is a vacuum in the center of my chest, a vacuum that I cannot fill. Oh, and no one's sure of anything. I'm stupid.

I always seek happiness but never seem to find it. I thought that with the birth of my little girl, I was finally going to find some peace, a sort of balance in me, like a calmness in 'my urgency,' but that's not the case. I still have this void that comes back and bothers me. First, what is happiness? Maybe it's a myth, and no one is ever really happy. He's right. It's like an obsession within me. I cannot put myself in a relationship. Maybe I made the wrong choice again. There was Laurent. We were good together, but as soon as I wanted to go faster—the house, the child—he wanted to slow down, to think. He hoped that I would be less excessive, and he did not approve of this fury in me, this love of excesses. According to him, I needed to be more grounded, to slow down. I know I miss him. I should have....

"Sometimes I still meet him at the salon, and then I feel a rush of sadness for breaking up with him on a whim. I'm full of regret, and it always gives me a stomachache. I understand it is so hard to live."

A few tears began to run down Cindy's cheeks, as if to wash away her anger. She glanced briefly in the rear-view mirror to see if her makeup was messed up, and in that moment she lost control of the car. She was driving so fast. She tried to get back on the road, but she was unable to avoid a tree near a house. The shock was inevitable. It was extremely violent.

For Cindy, there was a very strong blow, a sharp pain, nausea, and then nothing.

She was no more than a lifeless body, and yet the ethereal form of her consciousness was standing a few feet from the shattered car, watching the carcass embedded in the tree. Cindy was certain she had been ejected during the impact. Soon, other vehicles arrived at the scene.

Sometime later, from soul to soul, here is what she disclosed to me:

70

"People began to gather around what was left of my car, and, like them, I approached. I had the feeling of floating while moving. Maybe I was hurt more than I thought? My only concern then was contacting my family and colleagues, to reassure them. Strangely, nobody seemed to pay attention to me. I was transparent. I watched with astonishment as the paramedics and firefighters tried to pull a human body from my car. Who could it be? Since I was right here, I was more and more confused. I looked at my hands, my body. I touched my head. Yes, I was there and alive and well. I walked away along the side of the road to rest and reflect on the last moments before the collision. A maneuver, a distraction, and here I am. I found myself against this tree. I needed help getting my car off the road. I remember that my body, still numb and nauseated, suddenly felt surrounded by a terrible mist. I could not see even one meter ahead, and I was stuck on this road, unable to make contact with anyone.

My family was going to worry. Fortunately, they knew the place. They would certainly come to get me and help me out."

Four days passed, and Cindy was still near her car. At least, she thought she was there. In actuality, it had been many days since her car had been towed away, and her funerals were going to take place soon. But how could she realize this when she saw herself as alive? Cindy was far from understanding that her death had already created intense upheavals. In her head, everything was confused. She began to go between the scene of the accident and strange scenes of funerals, where she saw her family crying. But why were they all crying? Whose body were they accompanying? Hers? Of course not. That was not her! She was among them, with her mother, her father, her little daughter, her spouse, and her friends. Yet in their thoughts, it was her name that resonated, her name that she heard. What was happening?

Cindy was trying to talk to them, to tell them there had been a mistake, that she was alive and just needed help on the road near her car. Would they finally understand that this body they were burying was not hers?[13]

A week after the funerals, a close friend of Cindy's who had heard about me sent me a picture of her. His note said he felt she was not well and that he was certain she needed help where she was because she was not in the Light.

I agreed to join Cindy in an out-of-body projection, because my first attempts at telepathic contact with her with the help of the photo had failed.

It was predictable: Cindy didn't know me. I understood that her soul needed comfort and explanations. Finally, calling the Light to me, I came to her. Cindy was still there, very close to her car in the "airlock" of mental energy that she had created unconsciously to take refuge in. Her "bubble" was a greenish-yellow color. I could see some of her crazy thoughts and the image of a nearby field. In a loop, Cindy was leaving through the only door still intact on her destroyed car, walking around the car, watching the tree damaged by the car, and returning to sit again in what was left of her vehicle, on the passenger side.

Wearing a black wool sweater and jeans, this young woman was beautiful, with her red hair and soft blue eyes. It was painful for me to see her doing rounds on "her" side of the road with no purpose and no end.

It was clear that Cindy had become totally bogged down inside her inner repetitive time, and she could no longer pin anything down. Obviously, I would never be able to touch her like this.

So many souls have not opened themselves up to the possibility of the Afterlife. Such a soul lives in deep distress and experiences a kind of panic when death occurs.

If the being does not believe in the survival of the consciousness after death, it is this "nothing there" that presents itself to him once he has himself "passed through the Door."

We are talking about a perverse trap that the soul constructs—a virtual space—into which she sinks, locked in a kind of mental glue, unable to open her eyes to the presence of the guides ready to welcome her and introduce her to new horizons.

I have noticed that for these souls, time matters little because the soul always gets to a point of opening up and "seeing." Whether it takes a month, two months, a year, or a century of earthly time, the soul will always manage to break out of its impasse with "great love strokes."

But helping without delay is what I try to do because I think it is imperative to act as quickly as possible to aid in breaking her circle of self-isolation and withdrawal. This prevents the stagnation of the soul. It's not an easy job, but it must be done, as much to liberate the family as the deceased.

"Cindy! Cindy!" I called out.

Nothing worked. The young woman did not even turn around. Instead, she continued her repetitive pattern. On three occasions, I joined her in vain before finally realizing that she needed to hear a name she knew. I had to create a point of reference that would then lead her to listen to me and trust me. I went back to her a fourth time.

This time, I firmly told her, "Cindy, listen to me. Laurent sent me. He knows that you need help, and I have come to help you on his behalf. Look at me. Look at me!"

Cindy finally stopped running in circles and slowly turned to me. Her eyes were wide, her expression livid. She was totally immobilized, and upon realizing I was nearby, she questioned me.

"Laurent? Do you know him? How does he know I had a car accident and can't get out of my car? I went to ask for help from my family, but they think I'm dead. They had funerals, but it was not me. It's not possible! They are wrong. I'm still here. Can you tell them that you see me and hear me?"

"Cindy, listen to me: You did not survive the impact of your car accident. You're dead, and it was your funerals that you saw. Your loved ones cannot hear you because you don't have your body of flesh anymore. You have a Body of Light, and you have to continue to live. You live! You are alive!"

"So, this is true? I am dead? Really dead?" she asked me emphatically, starting to cry loudly.

"Yes, and I must repeat it to you. You died from your life on Earth with your terrestrial family. But look, you keep thinking, you see me, you move. You live, right?"

"A life? Do you call it a life, that of a ghost? I do not want that role! Keep it for yourself. You're the ghost. My little girl—what will she become without me? I cannot accept this! I want to see my family again. Do something!"

"Cindy, I cannot change anything, unfortunately. Your loved ones will keep your memory in their hearts, and you will watch over them. This can be a very nice role. Death, you see, is simply another channel through which life expresses itself. You know, like TV channels when you flip through them? Well, it's a little bit of the same thing."

Cindy stared at me. She was furious and visibly stifled anger she could not express. Gray wreaths surrounded both of us, showing the level of suffering in her soul. In the depths of her impasse, the young woman could not find words.

"I don't want this! I don't want to die! I never wanted to finish stupidly like this!"

I did not know how to draw a bridge between the two of us. Words are always so weak! I thought that maybe a little silence would help. I could return when I felt a real call from her, because I had come this time. She hadn't called me.

There is a balance to be found between what needs to be done and what should be left alone. It should never be forced. I had so often noticed this!

"I am going to come back, Cindy. I will come back when you ask me to."

"Don't leave me alone here! I am too scared!"

74

"There's nothing to be afraid of. Believe me. Send me a sign, and I will come back to you."

I found myself then lying in bed again, my heart heavy. How difficult this last contact was! Fortunately, I didn't have to wait long. Cindy's form soon took shape in her subtle state at the foot of my bed. She was already there, staring at me. Very quickly, she moved toward me.

"Please, assist me," she said. "I want to understand. This can't last any longer! I know you're right. I *am* dead. I am having a hard time leaving my life because I have the impression that my heart still beats. Waiting makes me suffer more than anything else."

Because the request was real and profound, Cindy and I were both instantly transported to the scene of the accident, facing the field on the other side of the road.

"Yes, Cindy," I said, "this car accident, this field. What was bound to happen did happen, I suppose. I don't know the reasons. No one knows when death will come. But your soul— your spirit—knew. Perhaps you even unconsciously felt that moment coming, like how you were living with a sense of urgency. Laurent told me that you wanted—"

Before I could finish my sentence, bright blue silhouettes approached us slowly. They slid along the grass of the field. There was no noise, just a breath of air, a feeling of serenity, a wave of peace. The blue silhouettes held out their hands to Cindy.

I felt her soul smiling.

"I don't know where I'm going, but I will be better there than here. I feel moved by an indescribable love, a love without judgment. I'm not scared anymore. I am finally well. I don't feel any urgency, only peace. I am not dead. Tell them! Tell my family that I will always be close to them. Tell them that I live someplace else, and we will all meet again one day. I am sure now. I will wait. I will have another chance. It's just a break, is it not?"

"I will tell Laurent. Your family cannot hear this yet, though, as they're not quite ready."

Cindy took three steps toward the Light, then ten, and the presences in blue surrounded her with their arms. Were they arms, wings, or rays? I was not fully aware, but I knew that she was then calmed. She would sleep for a while because there are places for it, and she would wake up and continue her journey advised by guides.

I informed Laurent, but as for the rest of her family, it was up to them to open up to the possibility of another reality. Everyone has a way to go. It seems to me it does not hurt when you want to take a step toward other realities.

"Do not feel sorry for her. She follows her path like you all and like me. Life and the Divine often give us the experience of unfairness or making mistakes, but know that any obstacle has a purpose. Where births and deaths are conceived and organized, we also learn and maybe before anything else."[14]

Chapter V

The Little Rebel

"To live is to accept to visit all the dead ends that arise. As for dying, it is never doing anything that can personally engage you in a direction where eventually you will stumble. To live is to learn how to develop a 'tonicity of consciousness' within, which will prevent you from falling asleep or bowing down at the appearance of a test, such as becoming a target."

— *Les 108 Paroles du Christ (108 Quotes by Christ)*
by Daniel Meurois

I was sitting near our big terrace among the trees. I enjoyed these quiet moments in the wilderness, with animal, bird, and frog sounds coming from the nearby pond. It was my daily meditation, a kind of communication in gratitude.

Night had already fallen when my cell phone started ringing. I didn't recognize the number. I do not respond usually to numbers I can't identify, but I felt it was necessary to answer.

"Yes. Hello?"

"Good evening. I am sorry to call you so late, but I would like to talk to Marie Johanne."

"This is she. And who are you?"

"I am Lucie. A friend gave me your phone number. He told me that you could help my son, and also my daughter and me as well. I live alone with her since the death—"

"And your son?"

"He died tragically," she whispered to me, seeming afraid to be heard.

"I'm sorry. When did he die?"

"Three years ago. In fact, I am calling you for him."

"You are feeling that he is not doing well. How did he die?" There was a silence.

"He committed suicide. He was just seventeen years old. His father found him after work one day. He pressed the button to open the garage door, and Matthew was hanging from the top of the door's mechanical tracks." It was impossible for me to not think of Emma.

"It was terrible for my husband to find his son like that," Lucie continued. "Since my son left us, this event has separated us. My husband could not live in our house anymore. It was too much! It has been three years since my son died, but I believe I can feel his presence. People who come to the house don't feel well. My daughter too is scared because she told me she sees her brother daily moving here and there in the house."

"Did you call on someone to help him, to clean up the scene of this tragedy and guide your son to the Light? He must not understand. You know, a brutal death often leaves the soul wandering. I guess you believe that."

"Purify the house? Remove everything, you mean? My husband immediately threw away the rope. There was no more evidence. But no, I didn't call anyone before you. We had a mass for Matthew at our church, and he was cremated. To be honest, I did not believe in spirits before. I love this house. My daughter doesn't want to stay alone there, but my job requires me to travel a lot. So I have to sell this house. I will not hide that it's urgent because we are in the midst of a divorce settlement. People become embarrassed when they visit the house because they know that my son committed suicide here. The real estate agency requires us to declare this kind of accident on the sales contract. It seems that it is the law, and already, I've had to lower the price enormously. Although the house is spacious, its past does not make it attractive."

"I imagine you now believe in the survival of the soul," I said.

"Well, yes, but I do not want to hear about ghosts. I find the word too difficult. He's still my little boy! He is not aggressive. He wants to live with us. Can you help us?"

"I will do what I can. I can imagine what you are living through. Where do you live, Lucie?"

"In Neuville."

"Give me your address. Can you receive me tomorrow? I would like to see the house first."

"How much do you charge?"

"My fees? Oh, I don't have any. This is not a job; I just help when it is possible. If I come by tomorrow around noon, will that work for you?"

"Perfect."

I slept badly that night. I was sad for this woman with the hard voice. She'd spoken of extreme inner suffering. Matthew had to absolutely be helped. Of that, I was sure!

The next day, I was there on time and parked in front of a pretty suburban house, all white stone with a nice pool in the back and beautiful landscaping. Among huge blooming bushes, the dwarf bereavement trees sat with their bright orange and purple colors. Yes, the house was attractive, but there was something obviously off to those capable of seeing. There was a shadow area.

A woman in her forties, with a face marked by life, opened the door. Her eyes seemed dim and colorless, and she did not smile at me. I had the impression that she had never really smiled—I mean, smiled with her heart.

"Good morning. Come in," she said, motioning toward the hallway. It didn't take too long. I quickly felt the presence of a young man behind her, near her left side.

"Come and sit in the living room," she continued. "We will be more comfortable there. Would you like something to drink?"

"No, thanks. I am passing by quickly today. I came just to feel the atmosphere of the house. Could you show me around?"

"Of course."

I followed her silently from room to room, always perceiving the presence of Matthew ahead of us, though I did not see him. I had the impression, then the certainty, that he wanted to show me that he was at home, that I was not welcome, and that he was watching me. It was clear.

"Can I see the garage now?" I asked. "It is this way, right?"

"Yes. Follow me. I try to avoid it. In the summer, I leave my car outside."

Lucie opened a door on the side of the entrance hall. It was the garage, a large, almost empty room with two windows. It had a terribly heavy atmosphere. A shudder rushed over me, and I immediately felt an immense cold.

"Could you indicate to me where precisely you found him?"

"I never saw him because I was not there that night, and I never wanted my husband to show me where."

"I understand. It is not important. I will find out. I have my method. Can you leave me alone here, please, and close the garage door behind you?"

I then began to walk around the garage, feeling with my hands the energy on the four walls. I have always been able to feel weak vibrations and invisible presences with my hands. I was made so "by nature."

Without difficulty, I found the spot. It was near the left side of the door facing the hall and directly in view for someone opening the electric garage door. It had evidently been chosen by Matthew, with the deliberate intention of hurting his parents very badly. I told myself that he must have been very sick to be so cruel.

Lucie was waiting for me outside the garage with a worried look.

"And so?" she said.

"I am just tracking. It's too soon to establish a contact. I will come back in two days, and I will ask you to let me be alone in the house with Matthew in order to do my work and help him."

I had just said that when I felt a cold breath on my back and vague nausea. Matthew was making me feel his disapproval.

"Yes, I agree, of course," Lucie said. "How much time will you need? I will do some shopping while I wait."

"Physically, I will need one hour at your home."

"'Physically'? What do you mean?"

"Yes. First, I work on the physical realm and then out of my body for the follow-up. I have the impression that your friend didn't explain to you what my work is about."

"No, not really. He is a funeral director, and he took care of Matthew after his death. Concerning your approach, he told me that you will help him way better than he did."

Out of My Body: A First Intervention

The next day, a Wednesday, the day before the second meeting, I knew that I would have to specifically target the area of my intervention, meaning the spot where Matthew had killed himself. I would have to completely encircle the energetic zone created by his unfortunate action and dissolve it. As soon as I was in the garage the next day, I quickly managed to find the exact location. It was on my left, above a wooden bench, along a wall. There was a big, dense, and dark hazy circle (something I call an "airlock"), and that floated about one meter (forty inches) off the ground. No doubt, I was there.

Very quickly, I felt the presence of Matthew. Then I saw him. He slid toward me with a scowl.

His expression did not make me want to approach him, much less address him. He telepathically told me, almost screaming, to leave because there was nothing for me to do at his home.

81

Matthew still had the face of a young teenager, with freckled skin, a few pimples, and long hair around his bluish face and dark eyes. He looked at me provocatively.

His hair first caught my attention because it was a deep, raven-like black color that contrasted with his complexion. The hair had, of course, been dyed. His very dull green eyes and slightly flattened nose completed my perception of him. The young man was dressed in a black T-shirt and baggy black jeans that hung down low on his waist. His pockets were filled with large chains. The Dr. Martens boots he had on, untied, finished his very studied "bad boy" look.

The portrait was clear. It was that of a young person probably on drugs, a "Gothic punk" rebellious toward any authority figure.

"Matthew, you know why I'm here," I said. "I came at the request of your mother. I am here to help you. Your mother is worried, and your sister is afraid of you."

"Who cares? I like it here. This is none of your business."

"Three years you've been here, Matthew. You left this existence as you wanted, but you still live, right? So, now you must go to other places, those of the Other World. Do you not want a place where you can continue to live differently, of course, but also evolve and heal from what you experienced? Some people are waiting for you there."

"Whatever! I'll stay at home here. Go away!"

Matthew left as he came, in a puff of gray and cold smoke. He dissolved himself. I understood that my task would be a hard one. It was predictable.

Thursday

On Thursday, I went back to Lucie's house at the agreed-upon time. I had some cleaning products in my bag and also a big floor brush, dried sage, lavender, salt, and a white candle. Lucie looked at me inquiringly.

"It's my way of doing things," I told her. "I met Matthew yesterday, and he made me understand that I am not welcome at all."

"You really saw him?" she exclaimed, placing her two crossed hands on her chest. "I made you come because my friend insisted and my daughter too, but I admit that I did not believe so much. I myself do not feel the presence too much."

"Can you leave me alone again for about an hour and a half? I will need more time than I'd planned."

Once Lucie left, I immediately installed myself in the garage, facing Matthew's "airlock."

After vigorously cleaning the walls and floor with the brush, water, sea salt, and sage, I finally began a long monologue directed to the rebel soul.

"There are sacred moments in life when an unshakable and superior power uses us as a path." [15]

While "sweeping" physically and very energetically the gray bubble of the vibratory field that Matthew fed constantly with the charge of his thoughts, I began to reprimand him aloud. I knew from experience that this was not a case to push something like, "Oh, poor you!" That does not move anything forward. So I began to shake him and told him how much he had hurt his parents, especially his father, who'd found his body.

"I know you can hear me, Matthew. I am not afraid of you. You acted like a spoiled child with this horrible staging for your father. It wasn't because of how unhappy you were, filled with a kind of toxic substance feeding your need for violent revenge. Revenge for what?

No doubt you knew very well that you were going to blow up your whole family with you. Well, you did it! Bravo! Your mother and father have separated. Your little sister still suffers from your act and now fears you.

Why are you persecuting them? You can't blame them for having given you everything, especially too much permission and money for your excesses of all kinds. I read it in you. You were the king of manipulation, right? I see that your friends weren't good company. You knew it, but you chose to follow them on a destructive path.

They did not follow you, though. You see, sometimes we are wrong. We are all wrong! Whatever you wanted, you had it, Matthew! Why did you end up committing this irreversible act?"

The silence of the young rebel crumbled.

"Yes, my parents gave me everything, as you say. But they did not know how to love me. They were absent for work while believing that their gifts would fill my emotional void. I was only seventeen, you see, and I needed them to impose limits on me, even though I constantly refused them. I wanted attention. It's not hard to understand, though! So, secretly, of course, I started using hard drugs and alcohol."

"Did your father suspect the drugs and alcohol? And the toxic relations with your friends? And your mother?"

"Yes, it's true. He tried to help me, but I screamed at him. He thought that my excesses would eventually diminish and then stop. 'Everything goes away,' he repeated to me. As for Mom, she did not want to see."

"Do you now realize how your actions destroyed your family after you took your life?"

Matthew finally appeared to me. He was above the bench, his face pale, his look defeated. He had lost his arrogance.

"Listen, I just wanted to try to scare them and not really hang myself. It was a staging. But I slipped off the bench, and everything went black quickly. I did not want to die!"

"Unfortunately, it's too late, Matthew. So you must now accept what is and leave your loved ones and this house in peace. You have better things to do and better places to visit. Do you accept that I am helping you?"

Instead of answering, Matthew stalled.

"Why did you rub the walls like this?" he asked. "Frankly, it's too weird."

"To knock down a kind of lock that you have laid here without noticing it," I said. "You know, there is a light in the hollow of life, and with your thoughts, you can tarnish it, make it dirty, and incorporate your sadness into the walls of the house. So here I am. I want to get you out of here, away from your refusal of the Light that awaits you. Because you are expected, yes. Let me break down this area of suffering that you have created here and where you are trying to take refuge again. You must live another way now because nothing stops with death. Look, Matthew! The gray shadow on the wall has faded. Do you see how the Light has penetrated it?" A gentle heat, a result of calling for the Light, entered the room just then. "There is a space, a world for you!"

"I don't know where to go."

"Where the Light Guardians have been waiting for you for three years already, three years of our earthly time! Do you realize that? Just trust and imagine that there is something more beautiful for you. I will come back. I will help you. I will accompany you. Do you want it?"

"OK, I will wait for you, but I can't make any promises."

At this point, I admit that I was totally exhausted. When I met with Lucie shortly after, she asked me how it went.

"Well," I replied to her briefly, "it was enough. I must confess that I too am lacking in strength."

"Did you talk to him?"

"Yes."

"And?"

"Matthew was willing to listen to me. It's a good sign. I will come back tomorrow out of my body to complete the work and help him with the Passage."

For the first time, I saw tears run down Lucie's cheeks. She'd finally agreed to let go of the hardness, to be deeply touched, and that, too, was a good sign.

"As far as I am concerned, I've chosen to come to the aid of souls who could not find the Light and were "wandering." I am referring to the souls of those who committed suicide; of those who experienced violent deaths or left in a state of loneliness; of those who were victims of homicide, collectively or individually; and of those who were aborted."

MJ Croteau-Meurois, page 9

"To all those souls who asked me to tell their stories, and to those I always, help, To all victims of barbaric and cruel acts, To the healing of wounds, the ultimate goal."

MJ Croteau-Meurois

© Elizabetta Baldan

"A 'goodbye' is never a farewell. It is a living promise! I indeed saw my cousin Véronique on the Other Side of the Veil, frequently and for several helps to the Passage."

MJ Croteau-Meurois, page 44

"Her daughter needed her help—that was certain—since she was still in danger. From her side of the Veil of Life, Emilie began to understand that she could still protect and help her daughter."

MJ Croteau-Meurois, page 116

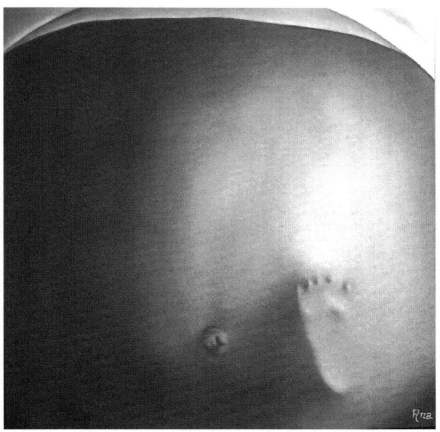

"The soul also observes the active presence of the Guides of the Passage, who will assist with the birth into 'Heaven,' just as they were present at the time of birth on Earth."

MJ Croteau-Meurois, page 12

© Marie-Chantal Martineau

"I worked with her for over two months, trying to teach her to erase her wounds and anger piece by piece. It was necessary to discuss this with her, to bring her some peace."

MJ Croteau-Meurois, page 66

"Matthew still had the face of a young teenager, with freckled skin, a few pimples, and long hair around his bluish face and dark eyes. He looked at me provocatively."

MJ Croteau-Meurois, page 82

"Wearing a black wool sweater and jeans, this young woman was beautiful, with her red hair and soft blue eyes. It was painful for me to see her doing rounds on 'her' side of the road with no purpose and no end."

MJ Croteau-Meurois, page 72

© Christophe Sauliére

Out of My Body: One More Time

The next night, I joined Matthew at the border between two worlds, as agreed. He appeared to me quickly and dressed quite differently. He was wearing a blue shirt and jeans of the same color. He was barefoot. I noticed that he had a blond or slightly red streak in his black hair. Everything was moving fast. I then received a gift that made me forget all about my fatigue: The young man's green eyes began to sparkle, and his pale skin full of freckles emanated a beautiful light. That's when Matthew gave me a big smile. A beautiful smile.

It was a sign that the connection had been made, that he was leaving, that he was a few steps from the new space, his own, where the Beings of Light were awaiting him.

After a few moments, he turned and gave me a slight wave with his hand, as he might have seen in movies. Matthew was finally delivered from most of his anger, and he was climbing. He had access to something else, to another life, to a place that would teach him how to be totally healed of his resentment, of his feelings of guilt too, and then how to move forward. Because nothing is ever finished.

"The earthly family members you have chosen, the souls you have chosen to find in this family, are not necessarily part of your family of souls. They can be parts of other families. There's no hazard. Hence, the urgency of healing the bonds with your earthly family, of letting go of old hatreds, old resentments."[16]

Some lines to meditate on:

"The universes are created themselves from each other. They live, of course, by their authors, but they are equally maintained by what is poured in them."

"Created from disgust and rage, you immediately generate a vibratory line of disgust and rage that will be added to other

souls of the same type. A world is always born of a collective thought-form—in other words, an egregore. It is the fruit of an unconscious complicity, in the light as in the shadow."

"The real comforter is the one who exposes the pain, the one who allows you to look at it in the face, then reveals to the other person enough strength to facilitate him taking an altitude above his labyrinth."

"Pity is never ascensional. She can only be a gravedigger. It shrinks the one receiving it and subtly smothers the one offering it. Pity is the simulacrum of compassion. There is not a single world in which an action of light can be undertaken with it. Pity can deposit a dressing but does not generate healing."

"Before helping a soul relearn the act of breathing, one must empty one's lungs of the waters of anger, despair, and lack of understanding."

"You know very well that a roll of the dice or a coincidence is nothing more than the argument of ignorance. Every life story is neatly embedded in a network of billions of other life stories."

"Thus, the arrangement of destinies corresponds to mathematics, which infinitely exceeds the most refined of human understandings. It operates in an area of Divine Consciousness in which the classic concepts of justice and injustice mean nothing."

"Every cause produces an effect, which, itself, becomes the cause of another effect, and this to infinity."[17]

Chapter VI

A Comeback

"Life... always tries tirelessly to sneak in where there is even the smallest place to be received. This is her first definition. She keeps moving. And she makes a growing field of all the hardship. The Force that moves within her completely ignores the notions of failure and success. Judging is too easy. It's a mark of ignorance."
— *Le Non désiré (The Unwanted)* by Daniel Meurois

There are lives during which we meet each other constantly. Sometimes, a soul reincarnates into the family of a friend or relative. They hope to catch up there as quickly as possible with what they believe they lost or missed in past lives.

This is what happened to a soul who chose a mother's womb in which to resume her life path that had been very painfully interrupted. The wound was too strong.

Ah, how sweet her first contact with Flore's womb was. Flore's belly was so similar to that of Louise, the soul's mother in her most recent past life. Her new mother knew some friends of Louise, friends from her last existence. I was one of them. What she glimpsed was wonderful.

The movement of this little soul into the body of the new mother made her feel at home, and so she began an inner dialogue with her.

Flore

A tall, dark-haired woman, a Quebecker in her thirties, was coming back from her doctor's home. She had just learned that she was pregnant. A mixture of joy and apprehension gripped the features of her face. She started talking to herself, as we all do so often:

"So, I wasn't dreaming. I really heard that little soul talk to me. She told me her name last night, Emma. I've always wanted a girl, but I had a boy. So this time, I'm sure, it will be a girl. How do I tell this to my husband when everything is so bad between us? How can I tell him also that this child who announces herself comes from a night of weakness with a friend? He and I were only looking for a moment of tenderness and comfort, and I never thought it would be prolonged by a pregnancy! He too of course. How is he going to react? He already has his own problems with his spouse. Why was I so careless about taking precautions? What will I do? Lie to my husband? Tell him that the child I'm carrying comes from him? That would mean that our relationship will have to continue for the baby and that I will have to keep this painful secret. I do not really like lying! Would I be able to raise her alone? My friend who is raising her children all alone is doing very well. I must first think, calm down, and talk to people who can give me well-informed advice, people I value who will assure me of their discretion. How about Marie Johanne? I'm going to call Marie and tell her everything. I love this little girl inside me, but how can I face my husband with such a pregnancy? Will I continue with or without him? For the moment, I do not have to talk to him about anything. I'm only eight weeks along. You can't tell yet."

Italy, 2013

I was in Italy with my spouse for a few weeks. We managed to combine work and rest often. These days at the

Mediterranean beach were healing for us. We had too much accumulated fatigue.

One afternoon, I received a text message. It was from Flore. I had been walking and didn't see her text right away. When I did, I knew it must be important. It had been a while since we'd been in touch. She didn't write me often. Life usually got in the way. I waited until dinner to read her message and share its contents with my spouse, who knew Flore well.

Her message said: *"Marie Johanne, I am distraught. I just learned that I am pregnant. It should be wonderful, but I am in a bad way with my husband. I know it's a girl. She whispered her name to me the other night. I've always wanted to have a daughter, but now I don't feel like it's the ideal time, this second pregnancy. And to be honest, my husband is not the father. The father is a very close friend of mine. It happened one night when both of us needed affection. Do I confess to my husband or pretend? I am not good with lying. I do not want this little soul to suffer from our disputes. I don't intend to stay with my husband. We went too far with our words. I also believe he has someone else in his life and that a pregnancy will solve nothing between us."*

It could not wait. I immediately responded to Flore to comfort her but also in the hope of keeping her from doing something she might regret later.

I wrote: *"Wait a little while, Flore. Do not panic. Everything will work out. A little soul coming back always consciously chooses her mother. Will you agree to take a moment of reflection and try to understand why she chose you while knowing your situation? That was three months before conception. Because it is at that moment that the choice is made, you know. I will not explain everything to you since we have already spoken to you about it and I know that you believe in this reality. What name did she give you?"*

107

It was late at night by this point. She will certainly write me back tomorrow, I thought. And indeed, the next day at noon, I heard the sound of my smartphone indicating that I had received a message. I immediately anticipated the answer. Something that I could not name within me knew it already.

Flore wrote: *"Thank you, Marie, for getting back to me during your vacation. I feel so bad. You are asking for her name, right? I heard 'Emma.'"*

You can imagine the shock I felt in my heart when I heard that name, knowing all the life that was attached to it in this new attempt to return to Earth. I dropped my cell phone and started to cry. I knew it was necessary that I convince Flore not to reject this soul. I had to tell her that we had known her before, just three years ago, and explain to her the circumstances of Emma's death, without dwelling too much on the details.

But did I have the right to say, "You must know something"? I was unable to contact Flore right away, so I decided to wait until the following day. Daniel, my husband, was as shocked as I was. We had to think of what we were going to say to her.

I heard two message alert sounds coming from my phone very early the next morning. I felt I was going to have to "walk on eggshells." I needed to comfort Flore, of course, but there was also an enormous sorrow in me, and I confess a little anger, about the situation. At her age, did she not know about contraception? I could not resign myself to accepting that Emma's soul might be rejected. She had been killed barely three years ago, and here the new belly that was temporarily welcoming her was preparing to tell her no, to expel her. I was horribly hurt for her.

"Hello, this is Flore," her message read. *"Did you receive my last text, Marie?"*

"Yes, and I must confess that you gave us quite a shock by revealing her name. I will tell you the truth. We knew Emma

and her former mother, Louise. Emma died suddenly three years ago, and the person who murdered her is still unpunished. We had a lot of affection for Emma, and we think of her often. In fact, the wound has not yet healed. But here we are, and she is coming back! I understand why she chose you. It's because of your sensitivity. Yes. Life is intelligent, but it's also a little bit cruel in how it challenges us. Do you wish to separate from your husband? You will be a young single woman then. Do you know that you look a lot like Louise? You know us. This is very difficult for you, but this is very significant for us too. What if we offered to help you? I mean financially and emotionally. She would be like a goddaughter to us. You would not be alone in this pregnancy. I feel like you are hesitating. Maybe you are thinking of keeping her? You said you already love this little soul."

"This time, I am the one in shock, Marie," Flore texted. *"How can this be? I am distraught. No, I cannot. I already made an appointment with a doctor."*

The pace of our messages then accelerated.
"With a doctor for an abortion?" I texted.
"Yes, in five days."
"Will you at least think about our proposal? There is maybe the possibility of changing things."
"I am going to think about it. I will let you know in four days. I can't wait too long. You understand?"
"Yes, I know. I am with you."

In the nights that followed, I contacted Emma's soul because I knew that was what she was waiting for. She was terribly sad and already aware of what Flore was projecting. I found her in a kind of desert swept by high winds.

"Emma, listen to me," I said.

"I missed everything. I'm still rejected," she said. "I am sad and alone while waiting for what will happen."

"You have every reason to be sad. But not everything is decided yet. Do not get consumed by melancholy and anger. I do not offer you my pity. I offer you my love. I came to hold your hand."

Emma looked me in the eyes. Hot wind from the desert blew against our faces, choking us.

She finally reached out and closed her eyes, tears flowing down her cheeks. I realized that she was waiting for the event, resigned.

As agreed, Flore let me know that she had made her decision. The next day, she would go to the clinic to terminate her pregnancy. She told me she was sorry but could not do otherwise.

"I know that it is hard for you and Daniel now that both of you know who she is, but this is difficult for me as well. I love her, but I can't. I can't!"

"I will do my best to be with you, Flore," I texted back. "Do not forget to talk to Emma tonight and explain it to her. This is important, very important, for her soul, believe me. You must explain to her with love that it is not her you don't want but that you cannot welcome a child right now, whomever he or she is."

The Expected Day

Joining a soul in the space where she lives is ultimately just a matter of heart. But Emma was angry.

"You see, Marie? It's as simple as that!" Emma told me. "You do not understand on Earth what happens when you do not want someone. You do not want to get involved. You want to silence the emotions. You say, '*I do not want it,*' while trying to erase from your mind the image of this '*it.*' This is not a small larva, this '*it.*' It is not '*nobody.*' I have a heart that beats in me, an identity, a soul. I live!"

"What can I say, Emma? Before getting close to Flore, did you ever think of the risk that she might not accept this pregnancy because her situation is unstable?"

110

"I don't know. I was hoping she would get over her fears. I was hoping she would already love me more than herself—that she would overcome her fears and accept the consequences of her decisions. I was wrong."

The contact with Emma stopped there. The next morning, again out of my body, I was attracted to an unfolding scene.

It was in a hospital in Quebec. In a surgery room, a female doctor was preparing metal instruments in a perfunctory way. I captured what was living in her. She had closed herself off from her emotions because she knew that if she let any in, she would not succeed in what she was there to do. In front of her, there was a woman who didn't want her pregnancy.

I started to hear the doctor's thinking: "If abortion wasn't considered a means of contraception, I wouldn't have to do this job that often. This is definitely not for me."

Soon, the blood ran between the thighs of Flore as she trembled. She was alone. There was no one there to hold her hand. She would never know I was there for her and for Emma.

Flore cried as the small embryo was expelled, piece by piece of shapeless flesh, into a metal container. She did not see anything of course, but I did, and I was seized by intense nausea. It must be said that an abortion is also a death.

"Marie! Marie!" Emma called very quickly. "You see, I am nothing now. I don't know anymore who I am, nor where I am going now. I am exploded. I am unwanted in the higher and lower spheres. I am so upset about this rejection. I was in Heaven in my lightness, where you can't perceive the risks you meet when you decide to incarnate. I didn't think about it enough. I was happy to be conceived in her body."

Days passed. I stayed informed about Flore's condition. Some complications appeared after the termination of her pregnancy, but fortunately, she recovered physically and emotionally. She went on with her life, and I'm sure she's

111

grown up now. Everything in life is meant to teach us, even if we stumble.

As for Emma, I did what I could to comfort her and guide her to another living space, and she is resting now. She is rebuilding herself more than she did on the Other Shore, in what is sometimes called one of the "many dwellings of the Father's Kingdom."

Stories occasionally stop like this, leaving you with a bitter taste. But there is no ready-made recipe for someone wishing to help a soul find her rightful place with a peaceful heart. Each is ultimately the master of the rhythm of his advances, his pauses, his impulses, his errors, his hopes—in short, his destiny. This is not to be judged by anyone.

Emma and Flore will meet, that's for sure. And I would not be surprised to learn one day, here or "Above," that there is an old soul connection between Louise and Flore.

Chapter VII

The Cocoon

"Listen, a life is like a cloud that condenses in the sky of the Infinite. A wind pushes it, disperses it, and here is the cloud that has already passed. It disappears but is reformed elsewhere, sometimes charged with rain, sometimes with fine mist, sometimes stretching under the sun to gorge on it and finally dissolve."

— *Ce Clou que J'ai enfoncé (This Nail That I Have Hammered)*
by Daniel Meurois

He had just turned fifty, and his life was well established. Richard was wealthy, married, and the father of three girls. He had friends and a more than satisfactory social life, not to mention the work he loved, law. He also had a passion: squash.

He had been practicing it for many years at a well-known sports center in Quebec. He wanted to be in good shape, and he thought he was. His father died of a major heart attack a few years earlier, and since then, he had started training and watching his diet.

"Better to take precautions with risky genetics," he sometimes said to himself. He was often seen on Sundays on Maguire Street, during the first days of spring, after the restaurants and coffee shops had reopened for the season.

Always with his beautiful smile, Richard was a bon vivant. He was also one of my first lovers. Our fathers worked together. They ran a pharmacy in Limoilou, a neighborhood in Quebec City.

At that time, Richard and I helped them by working part time there. It was a happy student job because we were all in harmony. After many years, the pharmacy was sold, and we moved on and met our respective spouses. A friendship continued, but life and work often got in the way.

Then, about five years ago, I came across an obituary announcing the sudden death of my former friend. The notice stated that he had died in squash practice. I was shocked. He was still so young and athletic!

In moments like this, you usually remember at great speed all the good moments you had with the deceased person. I had many with Richard—so many that I still today can see him smiling on Maguire Street. The sensation is so real that it seems like a hallucination, or that I'm seeing someone who looks like him. But to tell the truth, there is another option I'm leaning toward. I believe rather that it is a sort of "etheric imprint" left by his presence as a wink addressed to me. I know that many who have lost loved ones experience these "apparitions" but rarely dare to talk about it.

I inquired, of course, about the precise circumstances of Richard's death. I was informed that he had succumbed to a violent heart attack. Attempts to resuscitate him were futile. He was immediately gone.

A Special Invitation

But let's go back. About a month after Richard's death, I remember feeling my soul called to a place I did not know. It was a kitchen "somewhere on Earth." But who was cooking? I didn't know until the silhouettes of two men began to materialize in front of me. They were side by side and partly leaning against a counter. The first silhouette was that of my deceased father from a few years ago.

I was surprised to see him there, since I knew that he was moving to "something else" in his universe, his Devachan, and that his trips back and forth to our world had become rare. There must have been an important reason for his presence.

As for the other silhouette, I didn't immediately recognize the person. In fact, did I even know him?

Still, I approached the unknown. He displayed a silent anger and seemed totally closed to my presence. His face was cyanotic. He did not look at me and kept both arms crossed over his chest as a last protection. Obviously, he was not there of his own free will. Moved, I then addressed my father, always on his side.

"Papa, who is he?" I asked.

"Look better, my daughter."

I looked again at the man for a long time and then exclaimed, "This is Richard, Papa!"

"Yes, I brought him to you for you to help him. I know you can do it. He totally refuses his death and doesn't want to open up to his new life. I came to welcome him, but he refuses to advance further. Where I am, I now help the souls who don't believe in anything. I introduce them to their families above, but sometimes... I do this service for the 'Other Side.' You taught me that it is essential, and I know now, having experienced it, how it makes the Passage easier.

Richard doesn't want to hear it, despite all my efforts and the help of his loved ones. He needs 'matter,' and you are the only one who can provide it for him. Do you want to help him? I will wait in the living room."

And then I saw my father turn his back to me and go to a space that I actually thought was a living room.

A Chrysalis to Be Reborn

"It's me," I said. "It is Marie Johanne. Do you recognize me, Richard?"

"They say that I am dead. You too?"

"No. I came to help you."

"You are in my house here."

"Doesn't matter. I am the only one who can see you in this moment."

"Helping me? Do you believe you can? My whole family believes I am dead, and yet I am alive. You can see it! I cannot make them understand. I try to touch them, talk to them, but it's emptiness, and I get a dull silence. No, I do not accept that I must leave those I love and this house that I chose! I was so happy! I do not want this death, if it is true. My life is really over? Will you tell me the truth? I never planned anything or prepared for this. I thought this only happened to others—I mean, going off so stupidly and disintegrating. My little girls...."

Richard was quiet for a moment, and I saw a tear run down his cheek. I could see that he felt very badly because he was totally unable to open up to the world of the Afterlife, he who had never believed in the survival of the soul elsewhere. In life, he always rejected this idea, which he said was far-fetched. For him, someone died and that was all. We dissolve in the earth, the flesh rots, and it is a normal cycle of "returning to dust." Yet what disturbed him was that he right now "still lived and had emotions." What he had denied all his life, survival after death, began to impose itself as true. He had to agree that it was not a hallucination, a delusion, but reality. Death does not exist![18]

"Richard, you are alive! Do you feel it?" I asked.

"I think I am living a nightmare! How can you talk to me if you are alive and I am dead? It's nonsense. I am totally lost! And your father is also talking to me."

"My father is deceased, like you. He is trying to make you go toward the Light, the one of the Afterlife, or rather another life. You see, 'in your head' you are in a prison that you maintain instead of opening up to other dimensions, where life continues. This is pride, Richard!"

116

I understood that I would not be able to move him. He believed only in the physical world.

So I told myself that I had to create a material to help him be "born in Heaven," as the saying goes. For that, I had to "weave" an ethereal matter similar to a uterine membrane. That's what I did right away.

I can see you smiling as you read this, dear reader. Know, however, that in the worlds of the Afterlife, we can create "all" that we want through thought because that is the nature of the place. The Hereafter is made up of millions and millions of holograms born of the thoughts of the "dead." It is for this reason that there are as many "paradises" as there are "dead" souls.

And there are as many dark areas as there are souls who built them by not believing themselves worthy of being received by the Light or refusing it.

In an instant of compassion, I began to surround Richard's body in a pink ethereal matter that the soul can spontaneously weave through its willingness to help. This would be his vehicle. My father then returned to accompany his friend and was also enveloped by the same matter in order to better guide Richard in his rebirth and help him accept his new home. I watched them. They were there like two living cocoons waiting for their departure, two woven vessels of light.

But all was not finished yet. After making a very tight weaving around them, I felt a presence at my side. I had been helped in wrapping them!

It was my daughter, who is a Helper Soul like me! Sometimes, she leaves her physical body and joins me to help with disembodied souls. Though she is very good at it, she is not able to fully dedicate her time to her gift. But this time especially we smiled, and then we took a last look at the "vehicles" of Richard and my father, her grandfather.

"It is good," I said. "I think it will go well for Richard. It looks like he has calmed down and is going to sleep like a baby in his swaddling clothes."

"Yes, Mama. They are already in departure. It is wonderful to watch. Look at this sparkle of blue light around them."

She was right. There was so much life in the cocoons! My hands were still full of this life, which we often deny and that has nothing to do with the ideas we have about death.

As you can see, there is no single way to help with the Passage. Each death needs its own time, and each story is unique to the soul who lives it.

Chapter VIII

Pregnancy Time

"We are only two human beings trying to advance as best we can. Sometimes together, sometimes alone, but always as best as possible. Yes, we write beautiful pages of which we are proud and then others that we want to tear out.... And then? What happened must have happened before.... The freedom to direct one's life is also that of not always understanding or mastering everything."

— *Le Non désiré (The Unwanted)* by Daniel Meurois

It was a beautiful sunny day in July. The temperature was hot, and everything seemed to smile at Emilie. In the company of her husband, she left the maternity clinic of a large hospital with good news.

Her delay in giving birth was not an issue, and her baby was fine. It was a little girl who was just waiting to be born, a very wanted child. She had already been named Rosalie, and she was perfectly well, comfortable in the belly of her mother. The birth would be announced in the days to come. That's what the doctor told them to do.

A short time later, the young couple was at a crosswalk, waiting at a red light to go across the main boulevard facing the hospital. The traffic was intense at lunchtime. The light turned green. Finally!

Those who'd been waiting at the light began walking. Suddenly, a fast-moving car, its driver totally ignoring the traffic light, hit the group. It was unstoppable. It hit Emilie hard, throwing her into the air with the force of the impact. Her husband, who had been following her closely, was spared, as were the others.

A few hundred meters away, staff of the hospital from which she'd just left were immediately informed and rushed out with resuscitators. Not wasting a moment, they carried the young pregnant mother into the trauma room. They had to act fast.

The nurses were crying, all in shock. Emilie's husband and the witnesses to the accident were bewildered. Then the verdict came. Despite intense efforts, Emilie died, and they had to quickly intervene to save the baby.

Rosalie was born by cesarean section and then moved to intensive care. Badly injured, she was even near death for a while. She did not have her mom anymore. This is one of the hardest births that a small soul can experience.

But why Emilie? This was what everyone kept asking. Why did this happen to a young pregnant woman?

The accident was horrible for the young mother, the little one, her dad, and all her family. Life is sometimes so terribly enigmatic! No one ever seems to be able to prevent the unfolding of its events or predict the sizes of the tests it imposes—tests that often vary according to one's strength to face them.

"When destiny has a plan that concerns us, we are caught in the storm, whatever we do."[19]

Crying in the Night

I woke with a start and immediately looked around in the darkness of my bedroom.

It did not take a long time. Although I was used to frequent visitors, I still trembled. Near the armchair by my bed, a curved feminine silhouette was sitting, her head on her knees.

Her pale hair traced a path of light along her dark clothes. Who was this soul? A woman, no doubt, and young. She did not seem unfamiliar. I had already seen her somewhere. Obviously, she needed me; otherwise, she would not have come to me in the middle of the night.

"Who are you?" I asked. "Why are you crying?"

It was then that the ethereal form lifted her head, and I recognized her face. She was wearing a thin headband, in hippie fashion. It surrounded her like a ring of posies above her forehead. Was this not the beautiful face of Emilie, the person who'd been in the terrible accident I'd seen on the news?

"Is it you, Emilie?" I asked. "The young mother who died a few days ago when crossing the boulevard in front of the maternity clinic at the hospital?"

"Yes, this is me. I am dead, I know. I read about it everywhere in the newspapers. I heard the conversations. I see my own family crying. I am cold, and my baby left me. Rosalie is not in my womb anymore. I don't know why I came to you here in your bedroom. It looks like I was brought here. I don't know you."

"Yes. 'They' probably brought you here. I am used to it, you know. And I understand your pain, your revolt. You have seen it. Many people felt sadness about this car accident and anger toward the man who so violently ran into you that day. But you have already understood all this, and I will not try to excuse nor judge the man since it has been said that he knew he was forbidden to drive because he was taking antipsychotic medications. I would waste my time, and this would not help you at all. And you need my help. I see it well."

Emilie didn't answer. I continued to speak to her: "You know, there's always someone to meet at the ultimate rendezvous. This one was written on your life journey, and probably on the one of the driver. Nobody knows when his or her last hour will come. Rosalie did not come into the world as expected. She delayed her coming certainly because she had to live this with you, in this cruel way. I know. To conceive of it like that may seem totally absurd. But how else can I tell you that life has plans for each of us?"

A long silence finally settled between us after these words. I'd wanted to get straight to the point with Emilie. I then took the risk of shocking her a little. Though she had found a road in the Invisible to reach me, she did not know everything. In seeking the help she needed, she had revealed a certain sensitivity, a desire to get out of there. Unlike many, she was not in denial about her death. But I did not want her soul to close up and get bogged down by too much sorrow.

"There may be a way for you to get out of this anger, Emilie," I said.

"You tried to tell me that my life was nothing, that my daughter did not need me. I was so full of joy and love!"

She screamed in revolt, and there was a wild reaction in her eyes, a glow of resilience—a kind of manifestation of survival in the face of hardship, a desire to continue her journey despite the pain. Something in her was far from "sinking."

"On the contrary, Emilie! Your life was, and is always, of great importance. Rosalie needs you more than ever. You did not think that accident could happen. It caught you by surprise, and your little girl also suffers from the same shock. She is in danger, and she needs her mom near her.

But, listen to me: Even if you are no longer on the same side of life as she is, you are still tied to her. You remain her mother. Her life is hanging on by a very thin thread. She was torn from your womb in order to save her because we could not do anything for you. Imagine how it was for her! It was a difficult birth for your little girl, and we must heal her now—

122

and not only her body. Her soul also needs her loving mother's arms. Her father is at her side, but she is calling for her mother as well. You both remain connected. You are still a mother! You must bring her back to the world. Only you can do it."

"But I am dead," Emilie screamed at me, crying. "When I saw myself lying on the street, I did not believe it. I thought I was going to get up. I was hoping to survive, but no, it was denied. 'They'—I do not know them—told me it was my time to go, that it was a date. I know my baby is in danger. I am even more angry about the harm done to her than to me! I did not know how to protect her and offer her a beautiful and gentle birth onto this Earth. I was so prepared. And then look, she arrives with pain, violence, and the death of her mother. This is what you call 'life'? Is this fair?"

"The fairness of this situation? To tell you the truth, I don't agree with it, if we simply take a human approach, because it's too cruel! However, I firmly believe in rendezvous with life. Everything depends on the way we look at the meaning of life. Some claim that life is unfair, but it is exact. 'This is beyond our comprehension because it reflects on the big picture of many lifetimes, requiring us to stand back and accept it.' If I repeat these painful words for you to hear, know that it hurts me to say them because I can see what you are experiencing. I share in your revolt. And, Emilie, do not say that you did not know how to protect your little girl. You did as much as you could, that's for sure. You have been a great mom, and your body carried her with love inside you. How could you have guessed the outcome of this pregnancy? Your companion is here now for Rosalie, but he needs you on his side, even where you are, as he is with her day and night and bearing the immense pain of your loss. He is fragile at this moment and in a survival state of his own. He is now more than ever Rosalie's dad and wants your daughter to live because he knows that's what you would have wanted more than anything. Through her, your memory remains in him. As for life, the Great Life, we can talk about it again. Do you want Rosalie to survive her wounds and heal quickly from her birth?"

"Of course I want her to live! How could it be otherwise? What was I thinking? I was not vigilant enough, right? Ah, if only I could go back. Maybe I could postpone this test. If I'd waited a minute before crossing the street, it would not have been 'us' caught by that man! It is so absurd! Why us? I carried another life in me. We were so happy! Tell me, can I come see you again? I need so much to sleep."

"As you wish, Emilie. Let me know. You know how to find the way to reach me."

Mother and Daughter

Emilie came back two nights later. I already saw the beginnings of an easing of the features of her face. She was starting to relax and accept her story, one could say. She was no longer in absolute revolt but had taken a second breath, like an inhalation of hope. Her daughter needed her help—that was certain—since she was still in danger. From her side of the Veil of Life, Emilie began to understand that she could still protect and help her daughter.

"You are less tense, Emilie, calmer," I told her one night. "How did you change? Is it Rosalie?"

"Come with me," she said. "Follow me to where I am constantly now. I want to show you what is happening. I have understood things. I have seen presences close by my little one, and these presences have helped me too."

It was easy. I let myself be taken by Emilie's current of energy, and I immediately found myself alongside the young mother in a space of unheard-of beauty. The scene that then unfolded before me brought tears to my eyes. My heart felt like it had exploded, and I was dizzy. I stayed slightly behind Emilie, waiting for her permission to move forward a little more.

In front of me, a circle of light the color of a beautiful golden rose surrounded the mother and the little one. There was a whole universe of twinkling stars, like nascent cells full of life. Near Emilie's body, I recognized those presences that are called "Masters of the Incarnation." They were clogging the wounds of the baby with long silver threads. Their size was impressive, and their faces were constantly changing as they worked around the baby. Whenever a major wound was treated, it gave rise to small explosions of light emerald and gold in the child's flesh. I could see the silver cord of Rosalie vibrate. It was the cord linking her soul to her body. The silver cord testified that she was alive and had regained strength.

"Look," Emilie said to me, "come near. I present to you my baby, my little pearl, my Rosalie."

The very little girl opened her eyes wide while trying to touch the lips of her mother, who was bent over the tiny, oval-shaped bed Rosalie was in.

Obviously, I had been invited by the mother and daughter into a transitory space between life and death, where they could communicate. And as always, I could see that there was only life expressing itself.

"You see, I help her as I can," Emilie said. "From where I am, I send her all the love of my soul, hoping that my love will help her to heal from everything. I will stay close by her for as long as she needs to recover. I want her to live."

With her hand, the young mother caressed the body of her baby, and I saw a multitude of sparks continuing to act where the little soul needed it. It was so beautiful that I started crying.

"It seems to me that the whole starry vault accompanies you in your prayers and everywhere you can go," I said. "You're full of greatness, Emilie. You have moved me a lot. A lot."

"This is the love that I have for her that gives me the strength, as do these beings here with us," she said. *"I think *they are like Angels*. They were already present when I died, and they also accompanied my little one during her forced birth. I am convinced they will stay as long as necessary, and then after I will follow them. I know that Rosalie's father will take care of her very well."

Spontaneously, Emilie handed me her little daughter, and I took her in my arms. I had the sensation of holding a small bird, airy and fragile. I, in turn, sent Rosalie all my thoughts of healing by touching her body with care before giving her back to her mother. I was smiling.

"I saw the prayers you said for both of us on Earth," Emilie told me. "I received them. It made me feel so good. I also saw the chain of all the prayers and thoughts said for us everywhere. You will tell them? You will mention our meeting, right?"

"Yes, I will testify with your family's permission. I am writing a book on the subject, and you can be a part of it if you want to. Did you see how Rosalie's dad and your entire family have been hopeful for Rosalie's recovery? Nevertheless, they cry about your departure. They are devastated, but they are strong and loving. My physical body requires me to go back into it now, Emilie. I can feel it. Can you let me know when you follow the beings who are taking care of the little one?"

"Yes, I will," she said. "I'm staying here with Rosalie until there is no danger anymore. After that, I will join them. That's for sure because I too must be 'repaired' and sleep a little longer. Then, you know, I will no longer look for understanding about why I had to be there with my baby and my partner that day at that precise moment. You have helped in making me understand that there was a reason, a 'reason of the soul' that is greater than me. It is what it is, and that's all. The understanding will come when it is necessary. Anger, hate—they are poisons! It is sometimes difficult, but I try to move forward. After experiencing such a space of love near these beings, I am more at peace, and there is more light for me. I do not hurt, and it's even sweet. I will tell you when I go. I feel that it will not be very long from now."

Barely ten days later, Emilie drew herself to my side. How beautiful she was! There was no trace of wounds, and her face was that of a young girl only twenty years old. She had bright, almost feline-like eyes and slightly pinkish-white cheeks. She wore a loose tunic through which I saw her belly, which was flat again. She also had on her headband, always in hippie fashion, made this time with real little roses in a nod to Rosalie.

"That's it, Marie," she said, with a broad smile. "I am leaving. My Rosalie is doing better, and I must give more space for her dad. This whole story is sweeter now. I am at peace. Thank you for your help, and tell them that I love them—my partner, my family, and my Rosalie. They are in me. One day, we will meet again. I know it! Love is forever."

The silhouette of Emilie delicately dematerialized. Today, I thank her soul for allowing me to come so close to her during this difficult and unique life experience. I also have a strong feeling that I will see her again.

"The act of dying is not easy to play! Mentally, I did not want to leave you. I am still young to dare to die."[20]

Chapter IX

His Name was Francesco

"No one escapes the beings and the events that he has decided or agrees to place on his way.... Our freedom, your freedom in this world, is knowing what you want to do with these encounters—a blade pressing on your heart or a chance to advance."

— *Ce Clou que J'ai enfoncé (This Nail That I Have Hammered)*
by Daniel Meurois

A feeling of anger was with him for a very long time. He had a dull wound in him that he could not tame, and the more it hurt him, the more he looked for opportunities to numb it. Was this angry inner revolt a part of his character, or was it simply the result of his genetic history, a kind of inextricable old karmic knot? Francesco was his name, and he was the youngest son of a family of five children (three girls and two boys).

For sure nowadays one's genetic makeup is often used to explain specific states of "bad feelings." But it is also like a lock that activates each time you don't want to acknowledge your "rusty" interior. It easily becomes an anesthetic excuse. Then you find refuge in forgetfulness or denial and amputate part of your potential to be happy.

Sometimes, a person spends a lifetime looking to exit their mental prison by provoking themselves in the face of death—not by attempting suicide necessarily but by constantly pushing themselves into dangerous situations without being fully aware of the dysfunctional words or thoughts affecting the soul.

Francesco's distress had reached a threshold such that he could no longer scream out in revolt.

It had become that kind of intense inner pain that causes a person to take steps to not feel his own life. His was classic: alcohol and sleeping pills. He excelled in the art of denigrating himself, saying that he was good for nothing, when actually he had incredible potential and the ability to turn everything he touched into gold. But what can one say to someone trying to sink? Francesco was a gaping wound.

He was also passionate about UFOs. He often said that he had observed spaceships in the company of a friend who had also seen them and that he was trying, often in vain, to be heard by those who dealt with these subjects. Those people, however, didn't want to engage him on the topic because of how riled up he could get.

Some of them believed Francesco had been "programmed" with implants in his body, which made them feel like they couldn't intervene when he displayed some of his more excessive behaviors.

It's easy to "diagnose" and "denounce," but how do you answer such calls for help? Francesco did not know whether he could confide in anyone, though, without giving the impression of being delirious.

Luckily, he was married to a wonderful wife and had three children. His family had already suffered a lot because of his excesses. At times, he'd nearly reached the point of violence.

His wife always tried to calm him down and to reconcile also after each crisis because she believed in the concept of "second chances" and that she could, in this life, help him overcome his uneasiness. Francesco radiated around him an energetic field of mixed anxieties, fears, and delirium and felt unable to live up to what his family expected of him.

So he locked himself deeper into "his world" by telling himself that no one could ever understand him or help him. Although his brother, his wife's brother, and his sisters often tried to help him and encouraged him to seek treatment, he remained in his inner rebellion while causing great suffering to his loved ones. To him, this attitude felt like a victory over his own pain, but the alcohol in which he drowned was only extending a deeper and deeper gap between Francesco and others.[21]

The Last Provocation

One evening in August, Francesco was visited by an old friend he hadn't seen for more than twenty-five years. During a celebratory dinner with plenty of drinks and in the presence of his wife and three children, Francesco, always excessive in his behavior, suddenly choked on a big piece of meat. He fell forward onto his plate, causing a huge fright. Francesco's wife, his friend, and one of his sons tried to reanimate him but were unsuccessful. Francesco died.

After dying, a soul sometimes remains stuck around the people they love until they are able to resolve issues surrounding their departure. These are souls who, like accident victims, cannot move on. They are usually unable to cope with death and remain wandering around their people.

It is therefore up to the Helper Souls and the Guides of the Afterlife to intervene to help these desperate or reticent souls pass through the Light. Some accept the extending of a hand, as we have already seen, but others do not. It must then be such a soul's own decision, their individual journey according to their capacity and their level of consciousness, until they can finally open themselves to the life that awaits them on the Other Side of the Veil.

For Francesco, this was the case. He needed real help and to gain understanding about his sudden death because he was carrying with him a deep anger.

So the first thing was to start cleaning after his funeral. As his wife was open to the realities of the Invisible, she invited Tibetan monks, accustomed to that, to "cleanse" the spaces where he had lived. On my side, notified by his brother, I went out of my body to join Francesco where he was likely waiting. I'd known him casually and found him behind his chair at the end of the table, his back half-turned, his face in profile. I could immediately see his emaciated features, his appearance completely closed. How could he receive what I wanted him to understand? With his beautiful black curls and fragile neck, I felt he was deeply troubled to have this time failed at his favorite game: defying death.

Death had finally won. How could he be surprised about it? He'd called on death constantly, often unconsciously, to free him. It finally answered his call. But, like many others, Francesco did not feel dead. I paid him three visits without anything moving. He remained there, in his house or in front of it, contemplating what was left of his life now that he was gone. He seemed to be out of place. During my fourth visit, something finally happened. He had realized what had occurred. Francesco then began a real telepathic dialogue with me. For him, the time to speak came when he suddenly understood that he had to empty himself of a sort of overflow.

It was obvious that he had been carrying a burden from infancy that did not belong to him. This weight came from his father, who had been very unwell. It was a long story from father to son, from generation to generation, as can happen in many families—a dramatically classic story.

Sufferings easily become like true "relays"—passed from soul to soul in seemingly endless races. It is essential to break such "threads of misfortune" so that those who remain do not perpetuate the patterns again and again, as heirs of the traumas carried by their ancestors. And that was what Francesco had perhaps finally understood, in his loneliness between two worlds.

It seemed to me that he began to integrate it urgently with the desire to adjust his genetic "node." He quickly told me about his guilt. Evidently, he now wished to break the pattern so that his children would not experience the burden of their family's baggage, the origins of which were lost in time. Francesco knew that it was important to get rid of it, especially for his eldest son, who was struggling with his departure. It was therefore for the sake of his family that he decided to say things, to tell his story. He knew that nothing in me would judge him.

"OK, I am dead," he said. "OK. I understand. I was told how it is. OK. Look, maybe it's too late now, but I'm going to free myself for my kids. I have to empty my bag. That's right. They must have told you that my childhood was very difficult. I never wanted to think about it or talk about it, but I suffered a lot because of loneliness and a lack of appreciation for myself. Right or wrong, I felt abandoned early in my life because I had to become responsible like an adult when I was still a young boy. A kid, as I said! I might have liked to study, go to school longer. I don't know. But I felt pressured by the urgency of running away. You know, I do not want to blame my father or my mother. It's true that they did what they could, despite their own suffering and shortcomings. But what they had, what they lived, their memories of the war—well, it had all become so unbearable that I wanted to leave the house quickly to roam freely. It was an illusory freedom, that's for sure. I was not strong enough to face my fears, my insecurities, and I did not see my imbalance. And my father's life especially, with his endless sufferings, created a big emptiness inside me. I blamed him. I was really mad at him because of the trauma I experienced as a kid. With all this, he marked me for life. I was unable to escape it! So, to hide it, I repeated pieces of his story, his way of being, unwittingly or rather without realizing it myself. *My way of being.*"

Francesco was having trouble continuing. So I decided to intervene.
"That's why you were the 'tough guy'?"

133

"For sure," he answered. "As you said, I created an armor of 'tough guy,' like 'untouchable,' because I couldn't look at myself. It is what it is. I played the one who was always right, with nothing to lose, and especially not afraid of anything. I played the guy who couldn't express any sadness, which I buried deep within me. I kept these bad feelings so hidden that I eventually couldn't remember how it had all started.

They said that I had bad behaviors, that I drank too much. I can't tell how much time has passed because there are no more days and nights here, but I am sure that it was not a long time ago. I must confess that my inner violence became out of control. I never bit anyone, but I manipulated and I provoked out of habit, and I refused help that was given to me. I had to be the strongest in this game! My revolt always fed me. Do you understand? It was clear for a long time. My rebellion had finally attracted attention. Really, it was a way of testing the affections of my family to keep them under control. I'm not proud of it! Life was unlivable. I was incapable of having real relationships. It ended up creating such a gap between my family, my friends, and me that it hurt all of us. Yes, I played with death—wishing it would come, inviting it, testing it in order to not feel my guilt. I believed I was stronger than death. And now, look at me!"

"You live with an enormous sense of guilt when it comes to your loved ones, don't you," I said. "Is this what is blocking you? Are you convinced that you will not be able to go away without asking for their forgiveness?"

Francesco twitched. It was easy to guess which prison he had locked himself in despite his sudden lucidity.

"Asking for their forgiveness? How can I ask for it now? But if there were a way, I wouldn't want my children and my wife to suffer because of me," he said. "My life ended so stupidly. I hope at least that it will be able to serve a purpose, that the chain of misfortunes that I reproduced and inflicted will break, that it will make us think, and that it will bring a total cure for my children, my wife, my family. May they place

134

their lives under the sign of balance, tenderness, and joy! I do not know! I must stay in their hearts. It's their love that will allow me to move forward."

As he took a step toward the Light that had opened to him as a result of his lucidity and his love, Francesco finally turned to me, saying, "This forgiveness that I've whispered about since my death, they didn't hear it. So, tell them that I didn't want this. It was not my intention. I regret everything, and they need to know that beyond what happened, I have always loved them."

Today, Francesco continues on toward understanding the vivid injuries hampering his healing and peace. He is also learning to go beyond the idea of "certain liquids" giving the illusion of forgetting. Beyond the time that flows and is measured in this world, there is a kind of secret inner time that is necessary.

Of course, Francesco is no longer pacing in front of his house. He left the physical realm to join another dimension that matches the size of his heart.

As he expressed it, the love of his people helped him to reconcile with himself. This is what will allow him to dissolve the karmic mechanics of suffering in which he has been caught. Despite the company of the guides, he still lives close to Earth, and he continues the real work of self-liberation. I know he will get there.

"There is never a place, a body, or a heart too dark and wounded for a tender light to visit."[22]

Chapter X

I Don't Want to Die!

"Not every soul is ready to leave the earth plane and enter the White Light. Some believe that they need to stay near those they love to help them mourn or better understand some of the issues associated with death. The souls who stay away from the White Light are troubled souls, unable to move on. They are unable to cope with their deaths, and they are considered ghosts."
— *L'Ame est éternelle (The Soul Is Eternal)* by Lisa Williams

In February 1986, Maurice was treated for a melanoma of the optic nerve. The news of his illness had felt like a real catastrophe in his life. He had lost a young son to cancer a few years earlier, and just the word "cancer" made him fall back into intense sadness.

He was also the godfather of my daughter, and coincidentally his first symptoms and vision problems manifested on the day of her baptism. At first, he reacted very well to the treatments for his melanoma, so much so that he was quickly declared to be in remission.

From birth, my daughter was a real source of joy for Maurice and his wife. They saw her regularly, and sometimes she slept over at their house.

Eight years passed happily for us all, and then one day, Maurice felt stomach pains. After a number of tests, his doctor told him coldly that it was a recurrence of cancer. The disease had moved to the liver, giving him a life expectancy of about six months. This announcement was, in Maurice's own words, "a stab in the stomach."

With his family, I began to help him in all his efforts to overcome the disease. We went to the best hospitals in the United States that offered innovative treatments for this type of cancer.

Maurice kept going not for six months but for two years. During this time, though, he used up the last of his inner reserves and was unable to accept that his life was coming to an end.

He had no personal path. "How can you accept death when you know that there is nothing after it?" he would ask himself.

For the last few weeks before his impending departure, Maurice's family was exhausted and could not provide adequate care for his growing needs. It was understandable. His family made the decision to admit him to a hospice facility, an "end-of-life house," against his will.

The hospice staff had to tie Maurice to his bed because of outbursts, prolonging his revolt and his suffering. Where was the listening, the compassion? Was it really Maurice who was closed? There was nobody to really take care of him or offer him a spiritual way to open up to a few suggested possibilities. I tried on my side to induce certain "things" at his bedside, but his family rejected my presence, I imagine because of my beliefs and experiences. They eventually decided to close the door to everyone, informing us that it was "what he had asked for." They even refused the presence of his mother, still alive, who naturally wanted to see her son at the end of his life.

Hurt though I was, I refused to believe this was really the will of Maurice. But what could I do? It was what they wanted. The family was processing their grief in their own way. And their way was to push us all away. We had to respect that and not force anything.

I remotely felt the intense distress of Maurice. Without truly being aware of it, he would sometimes go out of his body to come and ask me to promise him that he was not going to die. What an incredible request! What could I say to him? He just wanted to live and not think of anything else. I tried to explain to him that medicine and treatments would no longer work and that he had arrived at a door, that of death, which was only a passage, a transition. After that, he would still be alive but also healed. He responded with denial and closure. I told him over and over again that I planned to accompany him. Alas, that did not mean anything either. "Accompany what?" he asked. "The nothingness?"

Finally, one evening around 9 p.m., I received a phone call from Maurice's eldest daughter. She told me he had just died and that if I wanted to see him one last time, he would be placed in a funeral room until 11 p.m. for close relatives to visit. I immediately went there, and it was one of the most terrible scenes I've ever witnessed.

Maurice had been transported in his bed to another room. He was facing a crucifix, as if he had been a believer or because it "had to be like that," and a single candlestick had been placed on either side of his bed. His skin was waxy and brown, like that of an Egyptian mummy, and there was a white band covering his eyes. A doctor had taken his eyeballs out because Maurice had agreed to donate them for researchers to use in studying the kind of melanoma he'd had.

I was outraged at everything. I could see traces of the treatments that had been used to keep him alive during the last week, his last hours of agony. The ability to listen had never been there. I knew it.

After briefly greeting the family near Maurice's dead body, I found myself alone in the room, watching him. I knew I could not leave him this way. In my opinion, it was inconceivable. I spent a long time trying to help him free himself from his body, to no longer be confused by it. I felt a bit like a guardian angel.

For me, it was obvious Maurice was there and that he heard me. It was a particularly heavy experience that has stayed with me.

Everything happened very quickly after this. Following cremation, Maurice received a service that we attended at a church. The words of the priest did little to bring peace to Maurice, who listened from the Other Side. So sad! The events ended at the cemetery, with the burial of his urn. Why couldn't they understand that "the deceased" was still present there and angry?

Regarding what the priest said, I've always wondered why churches, for two thousand years, haven't been able to help people die better. A place in Heaven is promised for going to mass every Sunday, or there's "the option of hell" until the end of time. That's it!

That day, I was ashamed of this church claiming to be the bearer of Christ's message of compassion. There are so many things unsaid, and they teach so many lies and fears in order to maintain a kind of lock on how to get to Heaven.

Maurice had inherited all this, by rejection. In a way, I could understand it.

Time passed and passed. For almost ten years, despite many dialogues with his soul, I knew, without being able to do anything, that Maurice still refused to go to the Light. He was incapable of it. For him, what was the Light exactly? He wandered between what had been "at home" and where I lived with my loved ones. He visited us regularly. He regretted, he repeated, not having had the time to better "protect" my daughter and me. I would tell him that everything was fine, but he didn't think so. He felt guilty and only he knew why. There was something he hadn't been able to do at the end, and he kept the secret.

Maurice was not a "toxic expression," far from it, but he was a "sad ghost" who struggled with what he felt he hadn't been able to achieve in life: doing better and giving more. He had always been a generous person in his own way. But maybe there was something else too.

140

Then came the month of April in 2006. Daniel and I were just starting to live together. I had not told him the story of Maurice or talked about his regular presence at home.

One morning, however, Daniel looked up, and I saw that he had felt "something" in the apartment.

"Do you see it?" Daniel asked me.

"Yes, but very fast," I said.

"Is this a guide or a man or a thing?"

"This is masculine, a man, carried by a gray mist."

"Aggressive? Toxic?"

"No. Unwell, I think. But this was only a sensation, and it was so fast! How did you know that someone was here?"

"I know his presence. I never thought to tell you about it, as it had become routine. This is one of your uncles and the godfather of your daughter. I tried to show him the exit, like so many others, to go to the Light, but his response was to show me his watch and the number ten. It seems that our familial proximity prevents him from taking me seriously to help him move on from this world. Behind him, I always see a big white staircase. He comes down, and then he refuses to go back up. But since he came down, wouldn't it be that something of him has already "ascended"? It's difficult to understand. I want you to show me how you saw him."

I went to look for some photo albums that contained pictures of my family. There were many faces of men, all different but roughly the same age as Maurice. Daniel did not know any of them at that point.

"Tell me if you see him somewhere," I said.

I couldn't help it. I had to test him, and myself too in case I'd been hallucinating over the years.

Daniel began to turn the pages very calmly, one by one. Then, without hesitation, he suddenly pointed to Maurice in one of the photos.

"I saw him."

"Perfect! You found him."

There was no longer any doubt this time. We both recognized him. After this, Maurice's appearances increased. He seemed to be keeping a close watch on Daniel. At least, that's what we thought.

I do not know how many contact attempts Daniel made, but I know they were repeated many times. And always, he had the same result: "I cannot talk to him. He runs away from me. Also, I feel like he is watching me to make sure I'm not an intruder into this kind of life or familiarity that he has established with you. I think we should be together next time for Maurice to see that you approve of my approach."

"It's worth trying," I said.

So, on the Feast of the Guardian Angels, on October 2, 2006, ten years after Maurice's death, Daniel and I lay down on our bed and held hands to leave our bodies at the same time. Our goal: to talk to Maurice.

We made contact fast, but at first, my uncle turned his back on us. As we spoke telepathically with him, he gradually turned to us. His features relaxed, we expressed to him all our love and invited him to pass into the Light to continue his journey. Could he finally understand and imagine hope? There had always been a confidence and daring in the man he had once been.

A large opening finally appeared behind him. It sparkled, and you could see the white staircase, this landmark, running down to him. He then gave us a slight wave of his hand before beginning his climb. Maurice would be free. He finally let go. He was moving on. The number he'd shown me on his watch, ten, had been meaningful after all. He'd remained a ghost on Earth for a decade!

For a long time, I've wondered about the meaning of these last ten years. Why did Maurice seem to know how long he would stay "attached" to the earth, and to me in particular?

It doesn't fit with the classical schema of a wandering soul held in this world by a problem, with no idea of the terrestrial time that flows. Something was wrong.

And then one day, it came to me. Maurice had never stopped wanting to help me or protect my daughter and me. He had felt it was his duty. It was a fact.

After he left, how must he have felt about me trying to help him while I was going through a rather difficult time in terms of my personal life? What I believe is that, after his death, he was quickly contacted by a guide about staying near me for ten years, at which time I entered a happier period of my life. That's why he'd pointed to the number ten on his watch. It makes sense that he would want to play the role of "guardian angel," knowing in advance that it would take a decade before I'd begin my new life with Daniel. That is likely why Daniel had the sensation of being watched. Maurice had undoubtedly been "testing" him to be certain I was with a good husband and safe.

Maurice's strength in his soul enabled him to keep his promise and fly away precisely on the day dedicated to guardian angels.

Thus, sometimes, it may happen that a soul is committed to staying in touch with this world to provide protection that he believes he can offer.

In the case of Maurice, his faithful commitment stemmed from his connection with me in life.

I thank him for that.

"We are all, absolutely all, in the same place.... We only know by what means we go there. Even a trail sketch in the desert is a way!"[23]

Chapter XI

Five Months and Then Nothing

"Healing is an important process that all souls must go through during their stay in the Afterlife because of the wounds, sorrows, suffering, or sickness experienced in the earthly incarnation. It is not easy. On the other hand, it is a necessary stage of rebirth that the soul must undertake."

— Lisa Williams

"A mourning, it is lived to the end. It must be exhausted completely to go beyond…. The human being sometimes works like these batteries that must completely empty their energy before being charged again."
— *Chronique d'un départ afin de guider ceux qui nous quittent*
(Chronicle of a Departure to Help Those Who Leave Us)
by Daniel Meurois and Anne Givaudan

Why does life test us, from time to time, with situations so cruel and difficult to accept?

This is the question I asked myself following the loss of one of my babies after more than five months of gestation.

I remember it so well. I'd already said "yes" to the soul who was going to be a little boy. At the time, I worked a lot. I was in my late thirties. My first two children were ten and five years old, and I barely remembered diapers and baby bottles.

But there I was, having to start all over again, with a new dad. It all seemed very fuzzy to me.

What is there to do when nothing has been planned and a little soul invites itself, insisting on being in your womb?

For me, a woman's belly is a place for the "flowering of life." I never thought of rejecting the one who'd "knocked on my door," so to speak. Rather, I tried to quickly accept him and put my belly back to work.

The first two months were difficult, but very quickly, my stomach became rounded, and the initial pain stopped. To tell the truth, my heart was filled with love and joy being in contact with these curves. Like many mothers, I often rested my hand on my belly to convey to this new life all my warmth and my desire to protect him. Women who have given birth understand how a pregnant woman fuses with the fetus she is carrying, especially when she's aware that it is not just a biological being but also a presence, a soul. Every future mother is one with the being she carries.

My hospital work was demanding and exhausting, and I was anxious to take a leave of absence to aid in the good progress of my pregnancy. I was approaching the six-month mark. I remember having long, internal conversations with the baby. We were in a kind of bubble, really. Everything was perfect and seemed to be moving along. Then suddenly, I felt that something was wrong. I perceived that the little soul I was carrying feared his return to Earth. He was experiencing a kind of panic that I could not do anything about.

One evening, I felt a sharp pain in my lower abdomen. I realized that I was bleeding a lot. My partner took me to the ER, and fortunately, I was soon taken care of. At this point, I was about twenty-four weeks pregnant. I knew that if the doctor could not stop the bleeding, I was going to lose my baby. I was in pain, and I cried. My heart was pounding because it was physically responding to my inner pain.

And then suddenly, while the emergency physician was examining me, the baby expelled himself in a single stream without me feeling anything. The doctor didn't tell me, trying to hide what had happened. However, I saw everything in his face.

"I want to see him," I said.

"Are you sure? He isn't alive, you know. I'm sorry."

"Give him to me."

The nurse quickly cleaned the small, inert body. It was a little boy, and he was already fully formed. I caressed his little blue face and raised one of his tiny hands with my finger. His hand was still warm from my blood and from his lost life.

I was now alone with this little being in my arms. I had been left with him for a few minutes. I rocked him, talked to him, and thanked him for his presence, even for as short a time as it had been. I also gave him the name he had whispered to me one night: Antoine. This is very important; you cannot let go of a soul anonymously.

"I love you, Antoine," I let escape from my heart. "Even though I feel very bad and I don't understand everything, I accept your choice."

I delicately traced with my fingers a little blessing sign on his forehead and then I kissed it before the nurse took him away from me.

The medical team then returned to take care of me because I was still bleeding. I felt the cold of death inhabit me completely. I was weak, and I felt life leave me, my heart weakened.

After an urgent intervention, they kept me under observation because my heart was beating too fast, and despite the medical care, I was still bleeding too much.

I tried to rest between the regular visits of the hospital staff. Every fifteen minutes, a different nurse took my pulse, took stock of what was left of the bleeding, and noted the "results" in my chart. There was no sign of empathy. I was just "a patient in a bed" to them. I was "just a miscarriage."

Yet, someone did eventually make a difference. At first, I thought it was due to the changing of staff according to shifts. The new nurse who took care of me for the rest of the night did not look like everyone else. Sweet and full of love, she whispered in my ear to relax, stretch my arms, and breathe better as she touched my aching belly. The placement of her hand sent me waves of heat. It felt like she was chasing away the push of death, like she was getting rid of it.

"Everything will be fine," she said. "And for your baby too. Do not worry."

"What is your name?" I asked.

I was very weak and could only glimpse a woman in her thirties, with abundant black hair and matte skin, leaning over me. I couldn't read the name tag on her uniform.

"Ange-Marie. My name is Ange-Marie."

I can't recall exactly which words I found to thank her for her special help and support. I said something like, "You make me feel good."

She smiled at me before disappearing behind the curtain. Thankfully, she returned often until the early hours of the morning. Unlike her colleagues, who were automatons and purely technicians, she was a real gift of love. I will never forget the moments that Ange-Marie spent with me that night!

One week after leaving the hospital, I knew I wanted to return to thank her. So I went back to the emergency ward with a big bouquet of yellow and white roses.

"Hello, I would like to see Ange-Marie," I said to the nurse at the front desk. "She took care of me when I lost my baby last week. These roses are for her."

The nurse looked blankly in my direction and then at my bouquet. She was seeking, obviously, to avoid any exchange that could be considered cordial, "emotional," or human.

"There is no Ange-Marie here. Sorry," she said.

"Do you mean she no longer works here?"

"No. I don't know any Ange-Marie. We don't have a nurse by that name here. Are you sure of her first name?"

"Yes. Yes, of course," I said. "She said her name to me many times."

I was stunned. I left the roses on the counter. I hoped the block of ice that had just answered me would at least put the flowers in water, so that she would thank the angels in her own personal way.

Had Ange-Marie been an angel? It didn't take me long to decode what had happened. Yes, it was obviously that. I understood now! This Ange-Marie, who had so suddenly appeared and then mysteriously "evaporated," was, I was sure, the young girl with cancer I'd met and prayed for more than twenty years ago.[24] I understood why no one at the hospital knew her. Ange-Marie had died a long time ago. She was no longer of this world.

Of course, she was not an "angel" in the strictest sense of the word, but she had been angelic in her way of loving and therefore serving life. She had given me back what I had tried to offer her so many years ago. This is called karma. What you generate comes back to you, according to the most perfect law of equity.

As for evidence? I will probably never have any, nor do I expect any, but this doesn't matter to me. When love reveals truth, that is enough.

The least I can do today is thank Ange-Marie in my way with my testimony. This is the intimate testimony of a painful time in my life, of course, but it is also the living memory of a moment of magic. When the idea of the sacredness and vastness of life is embraced, such a moment is sometimes a simple blessing.

So yes, angels exist. Since then, I've met some of them. An angel can extend a hand when necessary. We are free to identify them or not, as they do not have wings.

As I have already said, I've long wondered why the soul of little Antoine flew away after nearly six months in my belly. I loved him so much, even though his arrival had at first left me feeling unprepared. The answer didn't come quickly. Life is a mystery in itself, and I think we must also accept that it keeps its secrets. Who are we to always want to dissect it?

Soon, the wheel of destiny began to turn for me, as it does for everyone. Sometime after the departure of little Antoine and the luminous presence of Ange-Marie, I broke up with my partner. Everyone moved on, and it was fine.

The years went by, and then one day, I happened to hear from my former partner. He had married, and his wife had given birth to an autistic child. It was a big test of course for him and his new family. It was then that I remembered a conversation from years before, in which he'd told me that he carried the gene for autism.

Things seemed to click. Would little Antoine have been autistic? Was that why he had flown away? Did he not want to put me through that? And if that was the reason for his departure, what was the link between our two souls? Even today, I do not have the answers to these questions, and it is likely that I never will.

A conviction, however, has settled in me: The soul of this child who could not or did not want to be born through me decided to incarnate in the womb of the woman who was with my former partner. My inner voice clearly told me this.

"Do not lose sight of the purpose of our present incarnation at any time. Do not be corks on a kind of ocean. You are captains."[25]

Chapter XII

An Autumn Evening in Vancouver

"Celui qui atisqua sinum, autem debis aut acceprature maxim der faceatur am, contres re libus ncipsam usanqui ad expelicto vlem reve evesit liburat pernate, officia, andipsae molut libus cipsam usem. Dieu and enisqui quos expecto libus."[6]

— *Vu d'En-Haut* by Daniel Meurois

Leonard lived in a small house in Vancouver for more than seventeen years with his wife. As it is for so many human beings, his life had not always been simple. He believed, however, that he had moved beyond his "inner ghosts" for many years now. However, recent events had brought him back to his past toxic behaviors.

From a very young age, Leonard was angry with his father. Born prematurely into a large family in which he was the youngest, he always felt rejected and diminished by his father, who, in his words, was hard and sharp. He did everything he could to leave the family home as soon as he reached the age of majority, so as to distance himself from his father's behavior toward his mother. He thought he was breaking with his paternal genetics, but he was probably already too late.

I knew Leonard in his early thirties. He had just divorced and shared custody of his son.

151

He was a happy man with a lively and mocking spirit. He was helpful and good company. His work led him to frequent the artistic world, and he loved to create with his skillful hands. It must be said that he had a good dose of talent. He was also a pretty handsome man, with black curly hair and golden eyes. He presented himself rather well and sold his services as a designer.

However, despite his strengths, Leonard had a bitterness within him that was slowly gnawing at him, and he knew it. Fortunately, he had many friends and a certain ease in getting in touch with others. He soon met a woman also with a young child from a previous marriage. Not long after, they bought a house together, and two years later, the young woman gave birth to a lovely little girl. They were perceived by their neighbors as a pretty couple with three children. With their artistic temperament, they were pleasant to visit with.

But there were financial problems related to the disorderly behavior of Leonard, problems that he added to little by little with lies to hide the reality of the situation from his wife. Soon, and inevitably, a multitude of troubles turned into a serious danger for the future of his family.

What had happened in Leonard's first marriage returned with all its heaviness and violence. In his dark moments, he drank and quarreled with those he loved. He returned to the bottom of his old anger, often delirious, until he provoked another separation. The conflicts, the words, and the gestures became too much for his second spouse, who, for her part, started to fear for her children, a young boy of five years old and their little girl of just two years. The family environment was, month after month, dangerously toxic for the children.

The inevitable separation was finally settled before a judge. Leonard retained custody of his eldest son, born from his first marriage, while his second wife was awarded custody of the other two children (her first son from her previous marriage and their young daughter).

They went their separate ways then without ever crossing paths. Leonard, for his part, did not try to see his daughter

152

again until she was eighteen. He made the effort at that time because he began to feel strongly that he needed to reckon with his past.

I knew the children from his second marriage because I was a friend of the couple, and I stayed in close contact with the girl born of their union. She kept a wound in her, silently but very present, because she struggled to live with the rejection of her biological father.

Leonard eventually met another woman, the one who shared his life to the end. Both lived very good years, even though his old ghosts remained buried in him in a kind of dormant state.

One day, Leonard expressed his desire to reconnect with his daughter. After accepting a few meetings with him, the now grown-up woman began to tame his presence and then started an inner process of reconciliation secretly with great hesitation.

When I moved, I left my new address with this girl who'd become a woman. I had the feeling that one day she would need me. I always adored this child, with her sweetness and keen intelligence. I never wanted her to again be troubled or hurt by a father handicapped by his own emotional limits.

The Past Strikes Back

No one can escape his or her story or the echoes of past acts. Sooner or later, one's actions will come back to haunt him. You cannot hurt a relative while living eternally in the illusion of feeling well inside yourself.

According to this truth, it so happened that Leonard returned once more to lies and his problems with budget management, and then the anger that goes hand in hand with that. And it was, inevitably, the beginning of another break with another spouse.

He was not able to cope with his anger or the recurring difficulties associated with it. He wanted to get out of his own way, to finally get out of "the game."

153

This is how he began to conceive of an elaborate, Machiavellian, cruel plan: his own death. In this way, he would show all his relatives the intensity of his inner pain, his suffering, and all his fear.

Leonard had been looking for a quick release from everything that had plagued him for so many years. He was very conscious of having been the creator of his bad luck and the reason for the failing of his successive families. He could not see any other way. I learned later that he was tired of fighting and felt almost more alive when planning his suicide than trying to survive the string of reminders that life hurled at him.

He wanted to disappear and end this life that, according to him, had made him a bad person who despised himself. He wanted to be done with it all. He could not even think of the sorrow he would cause. He was too obsessed with his plan. He was hurting, and he had to stop it, no matter what would happen. Afterward, everything would be over. Well, at least that was what he believed!

As I have come to understand over the years from helping souls who ended their lives, the idea of committing suicide is often like a parasite that eats you alive. They are suffering, and they want everything to become silent—no more explanations, no more conflicts, no more guilt, no more abandonment. Finished!

Leonard bought a product containing a high dose of hydrochloric acid, and then on one autumn evening that was darker than others, he drank it.

His body, of course, immediately reacted. Confronted with an unbearable pain that wasn't stopping, he finally alerted his spouse. She was the one who called the emergency services.

Leonard arrived at the hospital at the height of his suffering, so much so that the doctor first asked him if he wanted to continue living. Unable to utter a word, he nodded affirmatively.

After his initial treatment, he was quickly plunged into an artificial coma to allow his body to recover as much as possible. The doctors were hoping for a miracle and wanted to see whether his body could regenerate itself.

On the fifth day, seeing a slight improvement in Leonard's condition, the surgeon decided to operate in the hope of saving what he could by replacing the damaged organs with tubes and bags. Unfortunately, the doctor only found irreversible damage and terminated the intervention. Leonard was then transferred to palliative care, and his family was notified that he was terminally ill.

His daughter and close family members stood by him during his short agony of a night, stroking his hair and holding his hand. Everyone tried to facilitate his passage by offering him last words of love. Finally, Leonard died at dawn. In tears, his daughter, who still had my cell number, called right away and told me the whole story of her week in hell.

"Can you help him?" she asked. "It seems to me that it would be easier for me to know that he's accompanied."

"Of course I will help him," I said, "and I will not let him go until he hears and understands that he can and must continue on his way. I promise you. Please rest. I'll do the right thing."

Knowing Leonard, I already knew that this would not be easy. For him certainly but also for those who remained, full of painful questions, and his sweet daughter with her heart in tatters, a long process of acceptance was just beginning. Yes, she had begun to love him, to forgive him, to know him a little, and now he was leaving her in this terrible way. What a pain!

First Contact

I was quick to keep my promise. I could not do otherwise. I projected myself into the body of my consciousness, and I found Leonard where I was certain he would be. It was the place where they had deposited his body: the icy morgue of the hospital. He was well and standing, contemplating his dead body on the chilly block without even noticing that he was surrounded by other presences who, like him, had ended their lives. They too were curious about the flesh bodies and what would happen to them. Astonished and haggard, most contemplated their inert forms while moving the limbs of their new Bodies of Light.

I heard their questions internally. But I did not come for them. I did not have any concern for them at the moment. I did not doubt that they would make their own ways of understanding and that there were already guides for them.

The worlds of the Afterlife are, above all, compassionate.

As the saying goes, "Help yourself and Heaven will help you."

Leonard's form of light, oscillating and shaky, turned to me upon hearing his name. The expression on his face scared me. It was a mixture of stupor, despair, and also perhaps hate.

"You? It's been a long time," he said. "What are you here for?"

"To help you," I said.

"To help me? Don't you see where I am? Don't you understand? I took my life. I hurt my loved ones. I thought I would be finished with all my troubles, but look, I'm still alive in the face of my shadows! I keep thinking! Go away. I did not ask you anything!"

"You didn't ask me anything, but your daughter did. She wants me to help you despite all the pain that overwhelms her."

"Did she call you?"

"Yes. She has always remained in contact with me."

I saw the body of Leonard's soul slide against the concrete wall of the morgue. He was agreeing to speak, or so it seemed. It was almost unexpected in these circumstances. I approached him to better perceive the images he was sending me telepathically without his knowledge. My presence did not even seem to surprise him. His thoughts, frozen on his condition and what he had done, did not go so far.

As for me, I felt a coldness in my heart in this heavy and dense space where so many presences were turning on themselves. However, I had to stay and resist a little more before returning to my body. There was an open wound to be healed. Surprisingly, Leonard talked, ready to empty his soul a little. And against all odds, he demonstrated great lucidity: "When my heart stopped beating, I was violently expelled from my tortured body. I was empty of desire and full of resentment. It was very different from what I'd experienced when I came out of my body when I was in a coma. This time, a kind of cord[26] broke, and I felt a horrible fear because I could not go back to 'myself.' I was in the nothingness. I floated in the room while watching my family at my bedside. They were in tears. I had caused all this, I told myself, because of my anger. I tried to talk to them, but it was in vain."

"They tried to help you, but there was too much internal damage," I said. "Are you still suffering, Leonard, or are you now free of what you wanted to leave? I understand that you must have been in a great state of suffering to do such a thing."

"Getting out of it atrociously mutilated, diminished? What life would I have had? What a weight for them too. I would never have accepted it. I no longer suffer from my body, but morally, I am so in pain because of what I planned. I am in pain because of my failings, my lies. I've seen what my life was like. I did wrong. I wanted to die, yes. I admit it. But even in that, I failed. I have many regrets. I regret so much!"

Standing motionless in front of him, I remember being surprised at the ease with which Leonard managed to tell me what was devouring him. It was both hard to bear and encouraging—encouraging because it was liberating. Today, I recall the image of an abscess emptying. It was very painful for him. The best thing for me to do was be quiet.

"I was selfish, and my plan was crooked," he said. "I don't even know why I'm telling you that! I hoped, in a desire for revenge, that they would all suffer because of my death. But revenge for what? Now, at this moment, I find myself a little and

157

think differently. Oh, I know how wrong I was! I was blinded by my hatred of everything. I only realize now that anger consumed my life, all my life. I sometimes looked happy because I'd clown around to distract myself from my inadequacies, my dark secrets, my scheming. I did not lie, no. I changed the reality. I actually said what suited me. I made the story of my life my version, the one I liked more, and I ended up believing it. That's all! I punished myself for my own disabilities."

"I see, Leonard," I said. "Understand that you cannot go back, but you can heal and learn from your irrevocable act. As soon as one door closes, another opens. Life is like that. Hope!"

"Learn to heal? I am dead. Leave me alone!"

"I respect your wish, but know that I will come back when you ask me. Look, you're still alive and you know it, like everyone else in this icy room. Do you want to understand why you still feel alive? You will need to forgive yourself and make peace with your life on Earth."

Second Contact

Two days of deep silence passed, and then Leonard came back to me or drew me to him. I don't know which it was.

"They are in pain, and it is intolerable," he said. "It's my hell. Help me tell them that I was locked in a bubble of anger and suffering when I 'made my death.' Can you? I went so far into my despair. The idea of revealing everything to them or, worse, really digging in and addressing my faults was so unbearable that parasitic and destructive thoughts invaded me until I was blinded by them. I told myself that I would never be able to tell them how deeply I was stuck in a bottomless pit. There have been so many unsaid things in my life! I could not find a way out, so I wanted to disappear, to flee and avenge myself for anything that caught up with me. Yes, avenge myself without thinking about what could happen 'after,' since for me the 'after' did not exist. But I did not take a long time to 'wake up.'"

"And now that you know, now that you understand that you live, do you think you will be able to continue on your road toward the healing of your soul? Try. Tell me."

"I do not know anything at all. I'm so lost!" Leonard whispered to me before his presence dissipated.

That was all for this encounter. His progress seemed enormous, but it was necessary to wait and not go faster. Outside of our time, there seems to be another time, different for each soul.

Third Contact

This time, I took the lead and asked my soul to join Leonard. It was easy for me, just following his gaze internally so that the body of my consciousness could project to him.

I found Leonard at the edge of an ocean, an ocean that had given birth to him. It resembled the one he liked to visit regularly during his best years. He turned his back to me and watched the rolling waves. The weather was gray, and it was raining heavily. I knew how "all this" worked and that it was he who had invited this grayness and the water. He could not yet envision the idea of a bright spell.

Leonard immediately felt my presence and, turning to me, began to talk as freely as before. His face reflected an impatience, though, a nervousness.

"You again? Oh, if only you knew," he said. "I played everyone so much! I thought I was indestructible and stronger than anything, but I led the game against myself. I was filled with resentment toward everyone—my father, the women in my life, and especially myself. I was so arrogant! But, now, I do not want this bitterness in me. It weighs on me and attaches me to this kind of hellish consciousness, which is mine. Tell me I can get out! I would like to go back and try to change things, but I cannot! I know I was stupid, but my head was very sick."

"Was it your head?" I asked him. "Think. Was your conscience in it? What if you tried to forgive yourself by simplifying everything? You cannot go back. You know that. So you'll have to look up at what's coming up now. You are your only judge, Leonard. There is no other. And even though your family is currently living with anger, it will pass, and all your loved ones will eventually grow because of your unfortunate act. They will come to respect your decision and your silence about your intention to end your life. Believe me. Oh, it will take time of course, a lot of time, because these things hurt deeply, but one day your family will be able to lift their veils and mourn. Everything passes, and thankfully so! They too feel guilty. Did you know that? They tell themselves that they should have perceived your intention to 'leave' from your words, and perhaps your attitude. They blame themselves for not hearing your call for help, for being so deaf to your despair."

"They feel guilty? It was my lying, my secrets. But they have my difficulties on their hands now, in addition to experiencing the shock of the violence of my departure. I did not know how to call for help, but I always knew how to lie. I told you. It's not their fault. Everything is my creation, from beginning to end. What a total waste! I'm sorry. Am I condemned to stay in this gray space forever? Is this hell?"

"Hell is your own judgment, Leonard. This is you with you, you at the edge of your ocean. You shut yourself up in its sticky construction. So, listen to me. The more you forgive yourself, the more this gray space will disappear. There are people waiting for you to continue your journey, waiting for you to heal your wounds. It's your family in the Afterlife. Your mother who loves you so much is very close. You do not see her?"

"Is she here? Mum is here?"

"Yes, she is waiting for you, but not in your present space. You will see her only when you call to the Light and stop the pain and anger still upsetting you, like wounds that ooze.

Can you consider a little tenderness? Listen, my body calls me. My body calls me. I have to leave. Let me know when

160

you've taken the next step and will accept the hands that are stretched out to you, because there are hands! And above all, don't forget that you're not alone."

Strange Scenery

More than a month had passed since Leonard's funeral, and I still had not received any signs from him. Then, surprisingly, a call came without me making any effort at all. Outside my body, I found myself sitting on white sand by the sea. The sun was shining, and I heard gulls singing. It was not a dream. I was sure of it!

In the distance, a silhouette was walking toward me. It was Leonard, dressed in jeans and a pale gray cotton sweater. His black curly hair bounced slightly in the light breeze. He had been rejuvenated and resembled the artist we'd known during the best years of his life, his thirties. He smiled at me. A boy of about six years held him by the hand. I immediately recognized Leonard's son as he had been more than twenty years ago. Leonard had created the presence of his young son.

I stared at Leonard coming toward me. I was expecting words from him, but he remained silent. Then he abruptly moved to my right. I followed him with my eyes. A big door was emerging.

It created a kind of breach in the horizon. Surrounded by an arch of ancient stones, a staircase led to the door. I could not see the totality of this staircase, only its first parts. Leonard put a foot onto the first of the steps, which became all white light. Then he put his other foot onto the second step, which also illuminated from within. He was going up, and it was so touching to see!

Finally, he turned to wave and then disappeared from my sight. With him went the door. It was like one of those films you think won't be very heavy but reveals a deeper meaning by the end.

I went back to my body, stunned by this very movie-like transition until I came to understand the ultimate message. Leonard "the designer" had created his own scenery for his Passage to the Light, where he continues to rebuild himself and pursues his journey.

By modifying his thoughts, he projected the hologram of his ideal of the Light of the Invisible. He had come to understand "how it works," and he wanted to tell me, with the humor of his youthful years, of the hope found and certainly the forgiveness.

I immediately informed his daughter of his metamorphosis and Passage. I hope that with this story, written for her at the request of her father, she will find the balm necessary to heal the wound left by him. This is one of my deepest wishes.

"Listen to me. Listen to me. Oh yes, there is this wonderful corridor, at the end of which the sun awaits us. I walk through it. It's so sweet! It's an ocean of whiteness calling me, and there's such a beautiful voice ringing through it. She pronounces my name without ceasing, without ceasing. Oh my God! And I seem to have known her forever. No, there is not a moment when I did not know her. She has been within me for so long.

"Maybe you do not hear me anymore, but I want you to know about all the happiness here. I thought I was blinded by so much whiteness, so white. Yet there is so much joy in her, so much peace, that she is a dressing for all of my soul. I think I'm coming out of a cave, so long underground! I know all this! I'm going home, am I not? There is an odor that I know, a music also in the heart of the Light! But why did I forget that? Why?

Mom, is it you? Were you waiting for me?"[27]

Chapter XIII

The Day My Heart Stopped

"In truth, the question has never been so precise: What do we want? To learn to live again or become totally numb? Everything depends on how you look at life and how you take action with your free will.

"As for me, it seems more and more certain that the painful state of our world has finally a major virtue: inviting us to immediately let go of our egoistic patterns and superficialities by showing us that the only 'emergency exit' existing is the true expression of kindness and peace that comes from the center of the chest... in silence."

— Daniel Meurois

This is the story of Dominique[28], a victim of a major heart attack. The paramedics were able to revive him after many long minutes of uncertainty. After his stay in intensive care and a long rehabilitation in a convalescent facility, Dominique, his senses still heightened, gradually took stock of his experience and agreed to share the story of his NDE[29]. I present it below for what it can teach us.

Dominique's Story: I Was Dead, and I Came Back!

I went to bed around 12:30 a.m. with my partner. It was August 15, 2016, and we had taken a few days off in the center of France.

Although I wasn't feeling any particular discomfort that night, I couldn't sleep. Strangely, I felt like I was "floating." There was no pain or any precise symptom of anything, but everything was strange inside me, almost unreal. It was as if I were living within the intensity of my perceptions, which had become extrasensory. I was traveling a little between two worlds.

At some point, however, my right arm went numb. Then, all of a sudden, I saw a form standing in a corner of my bedroom, looking in my direction. I didn't react. Soon, it became a little more clear to me. I recognized my brother, who had died a few years ago. I had just thought of him that day because it was the date of the anniversary of his death. Immediately, I wondered if he was there for that reason or if I was imagining everything. Deep inside me, though, I knew the answer. He was there, silent.

In the early hours of the morning, I woke up my wife. I told her that I needed to see a doctor right away. I didn't know why, but I knew I had to. She asked me what was wrong. Unable to say more, I insisted only that I should consult a doctor without waiting because I felt strange, though not in any pain. I was deeply moved by the strong intuition that something needed to be done quickly.

We got on the road fast and soon made it to the emergency room of a modest hospital in the countryside. Despite my discomfort, I felt very calm.

"Where is your problem?" the doctor asked. I touched my chest with my hand and said, "It's happening here."

I was immediately treated in the ER, and still, I felt no anxiety, no panic. In the medical exams, the doctors found a blood clot blocking one of my arteries. It had to be removed as soon as possible because I was experiencing a severe heart attack.

Because the hospital was not equipped enough to treat me, there was only one solution: transferring me by helicopter to a cardiology center. Everything happened quickly. I heard they were taking me to Aurillac. I didn't feel anything during the trip, nothing perceivable in my state.

Soon, I found myself in a procedure room, still calm but forced to rely on my fate. The medical staff tried repeatedly to clear the clot. Then, at some point and for the first time, I felt a sharp pain shooting down my back.

"Do you want morphine?" I was asked. I refused. "No. No morphine," I said. I continued to feel calm despite the activity around me. I had complete confidence in those taking care of me and their techniques.

At last, a verdict came: It was necessary to abandon these particular attempts to overcome the problem because it was now certain that I had come in too late for a surgical intervention. They were going to attempt to dissolve the big clot with drugs instead.

Feeling peaceful, I listened to the doctors' voices. And then there was nothing. I heard a big buzzing, and I was floating in an unknown space. I didn't know where I was, but I felt incredibly serene.

I then arrived in a large, golden-yellow room flooded with light. The light in this room, dazzling but not flashy, prevented me from really seeing a number of silhouettes that were sitting behind a big, half-moon-shaped table. These were people, presences, and I was standing in front of them. They spoke to me, and I answered them. It was a dialogue that escaped me. Nothing seemed to remain in me.

What did they say to me? I'm sure it was important, but I don't remember any of it. Perhaps they shared insights about my future or secrets from my past. But why would they speak to someone incapable of remembering their words? Maybe it was something else they shared with me. Then, all of a sudden, in a jolt followed by a feeling of falling, I opened my eyes. A doctor called me by name. It was a woman, and she had just reanimated me because my heart had stopped. I had just died, but I hadn't realized it. I had been on the "Other Side," and I had felt so much more alive, my senses incredibly enhanced!

With this experience, I can and now want to testify that life goes on after death. And "death" does not exist as such.

It is not a scary thing. The moment of dying is an intangible threshold one passes through. Like many, I now affirm that it is simply a change of vibratory state. My death experience was sweet, light, and enveloping.

I often cannot hold back tears when I think of that moment when my heart stopped, and how I lived my death. How can I best describe the peace of those moments?

Death? I can say that I know the way now, and I can also say that the most difficult thing is not dying from this body of flesh but returning into it, living again when the Door has opened in the opposite direction. Then we must relearn how to exist in this earthly density. We must find our roots again.

The Breathing of the Soul

I've listened to Dominique talk several times about those hours, those moments when his perception of life and death changed radically to the point that now sometimes the right words seem to escape him completely. Of course, his NDE[30] experience is not unique , but I think it is still notable.

His NDE experience is significant because of what is not precisely described. And what is not described here is the moment of departure: the passage through the Door. In reality, this Door to the Other Side is hardly noticeable when one is dying, and because of that, there is no reason to fear death.

Dominique has always been very clear about this. He never lost consciousness within himself. His thoughts never stopped or even slowed down. *His mind experienced things differently,* and his senses were expanded.

His NDE enabled him to understand that consciousness is not subject only to the heart beating, that the perception of living is not blocked by the stopping of the vital functions of the body.

With his simple and direct words, Dominique has tried to explain to his relatives that life continues and that what is called "death" is a little analogous to dawn or twilight, when there is no clear break between night and day.

Death thus expresses a process of transformation, not rupture. As a result, it reflects the persistence of thought linked to the identity and personality of the person at the center of the experience.

Of course, there are a multitude of ways to die. Some suffer more than others. What Dominique is talking about is not the state of the body of flesh but that of the thought that inhabits it, of his perception of a continuity, and that you pass without perceiving yourself from inhale to exhale and vice versa.

You are never aware of the microsecond during which everything is reversed in your nostrils and chest, when you move from one side to the other, unless you happen to be holding your breath, like with sleep apnea.

Thanks to Dominique, I've often wondered about the possibility of there being a kind of apnea involved for souls who, for various reasons, remain blocked for a time between worlds. I'm thinking here, of course, of Matthew in the garage and Cindy moving around her car in circles.

The more I accompany souls, the more I realize that the individual decides, ultimately, whether he or she experiences an apnea of consciousness. You decide to freeze your consciousness due to mental conditionings—your attachments and often rigid idea of your existence not ending.

Dominique once confided to me that he's always believed in "something on the other side," and I am certain that this opening facilitated a relaxation of his consciousness at the crucial moment when his heart stopped beating. His soul probably never stopped "breathing" and didn't even notice the dying process.

Personally, as a Helper Soul, I do not feel entitled to say that we must "believe," because a belief or adherence to a faith, no matter which one, does not automatically make a soul lighter and more transparent than another. Such a soul does not have a kind of "passport," thankfully! What seems important to me is the openness to what I call "the greatest possibilities of the universe." There is trust and purity of heart. Do not close yourself off from anything.

The Secret

A question that might arise now about Dominique's testimony: Who were the presences gathered mysteriously behind the half-moon-shaped table? Were they Guides or Angels of the Light, like the ones I've already spoken of? Deceased members of Dominique's family? Let us not forget that he mentioned seeing a presence in his room, that of his brother, on the night of his heart attack, and it was the anniversary of his brother's death. Had he come to tell Dominique what was waiting for him?

I've come to understand that the answer in such a case is always individual, because each soul has his or her own story.

And then, just recently, Dominique's soul came to my husband and me when we all happened to be meditating at the same time. He invited us into a space of clarity, void of any decor, a space "just to tell his story."

Dominique knew that I was preparing to share his NDE experience in this book. I imagine that motivated his approach.

That night, he presented himself to us solemnly, upright in the Light. He seemed happy and even proud to be able to share his memories. "When I walked over to the half-moon-shaped table where the beings were present, I could not see their faces," he said. "One of them, after asking me a couple questions, told me it was going explain to me why I was there. Its voice was tender and warm, but I did not know whether it was a man or woman.

It was then that my eyes were attracted to a kind of fluorescent wall behind it, and I immediately felt like getting closer to this being, in a very fast, 'zoom'-kind of forward movement.

My entire field of vision became occupied by a huge watch, or rather by its mechanism.

I saw the many wheels and gears moving rhythmically with incredible precision. Then the voice started talking to me again: 'Do you see this clock mechanism? Take a good look at how all the pieces fit into each other with great accuracy. There are so many levers and small wheels spinning simultaneously that you cannot count them. Some hide others, and each runs at a different speed. They are different sizes, do not all turn in the same direction, and have more or less jerky movements. Why are we showing you all this? Because each of these little gear wheels is analogous to a life, a life closely related to other lives. Each has its own speed of rotation, its own function, but all are complete. They are all interconnected. This is all within the same reality, that of consciousness.

Dominique, today you are like this big gear wheel that is above the others, the one you can see better. It's like your present life, the one that partially hides the other wheels.

But now notice well that no cog interferes with another. Due to the logic of each cog's serrations, they do not "rub" against one another or disrupt each other's movements.

It's the same for lives. At the bottom of your consciousness and heart, you do not have to dwell on the movements of a life other than the one you're living, at least not foolishly, not incessantly. There is no need to look at past or future lives or other dimensions because we are exactly where we're supposed to be. If you do, it is possible that when jumping from one wheel of life to another in search of an illusory ideal, trapped by the nostalgia of another speed, you'll get caught in the gear that unites them, becoming like a grain of sand that slows down the fluidity of the mechanism. This is how a spring freezes, a marvel of precision is blocked, and a heart stops.

The wheel of your present, Dominique, has always been more beautiful than you have seen. Live and move gently with gratitude.' That is what was said to me. Suddenly with these words, I fell back into my body in the operating room.'

Today, I know that it was not just for us that Dominique shared his gift that night by reaching out, beyond his conscious will, with the true secret of his experience on the exact threshold of his death. It was also for all those who will read this story and undoubtedly recognize something that belongs to each of them: an instinctive feeling of nostalgia due to not being fully present in the now.

"How should we best prepare for our own death? Our lives may be short or long, healthy or sick, but there comes that time when we all must meet death in a way suited for us. If you have had a long illness leading to death, there is a time to adequately prepare the mind [and] initial shock, denial, and depression have passed.

"The mind takes a shortcut through this sort of progression when we face death suddenly. As the end of our physical life draws near, each of us has the capacity to fuse with our higher consciousness. Dying is the easiest period in our lives for spiritual awareness, when we can sense our soul is connected to the eternal of time.

"Although there are dying people who find acceptance to be more difficult than resignation, caregivers working around the dying say most everyone acquires a peaceful detachment near the end. I believe dying people are given access to a supreme knowledge of eternal consciousness, and this frequently shows on their faces. Many of these people realize [there is] something universal out there waiting and it will be good."[31]

Chapter XIV

The Importance of Being Able to Talk about Your Own Death

"Death is a subject that is evaded, ignored, and denied by our youth-worshipping, progress-oriented society. It is almost as if we have taken on death as just another disease to be conquered. But the fact is that death is inevitable. We will all die. It is only a matter of time. Death is as much a part of human existence, of human growth and development, as being born. It is one of the few things in life we can count on, that we can be assured will occur. Death is not an enemy to be conquered or a prison to be escaped. It is an integral part of our lives that gives meaning to human existence. It sets a limit on our time in this life, urging us on to do something productive with that time as long as it is ours to use."

— *Death: The Final Stage of Growth* by Elizabeth Kübler-Ross

"Do we die as we lived? My friend wants to know what I think. I don't have an answer. I have seen people who called themselves believers lose faith in death's door, and others who did not believe who found it when dying."

— *Intimate Death* by Marie de Hennezel

Dear readers, it is through these quotes that I begin this chapter about the importance of learning to die when you are still fully alive and aware in this world.

Far too many people still die fearing the "forced Passage." They are angry and apprehensive about it.

Many people wonder about what will happen to them without suspecting that everything depends on them. As for those who are believers or churchgoers, I must note that religion has surprisingly kept them in ignorance and fear of the Afterlife.

Organized religion has promoted guilt and blame among followers while positioning itself as the absolute judge of us all, which is childish in my opinion.

A priest takes the load of the "sins" of his flock through mere confession? Do you think that is sensible?

I see the manipulation of mankind into fearing the force we call "God," who selects "the good" from "the bad" and damns the latter to eternal hell.

What a drama! Two thousand years after Christ, it now seems obvious to me that there has been a distortion, misappropriation, and impoverishment of his message of hope and compassion.

As religion has offered so little help in understanding the real phenomenon of death, it is not surprising that places of worship are becoming empty and that, in the West, we have lost all sense of the Sacred.

A real spiritual process begins not with blind adherence to established earthly beliefs but through the psychic functioning of the human being and traversing the worlds of the Beyond.

Perhaps we should finally be taught why the Light is our fundamental food and that it is well beyond morality and faith.

Only your own conscience will send you back your right image when you leave this life.

It seems to me appropriate to add to this book the next chapter, containing the testimonies of various people I appreciate. I will include mine at the end. I am convinced that these reflections will bring you other information that, with its nuances, will complete mine. Even though some describe different paths, you will find that they are always in symbiosis with my approach and perception of the Afterlife. Everything complements everything else, and I warmly thank these people for their participation.

In order to guide them, I asked this simple question:

How do you envision your own death and what follows?

"I am convinced that understanding what happens after death is just as important—if not more important—than what happens at the moment of death. Why? Because this 'after' depends on your 'before'—that is, your 'now' or every moment of your life that flows.

"In the same way that a dream will reflect certain aspects of your inner world, what we generally call the Beyond is exactly the elements that populate your heart and mind. Implicitly, it means that there is not a world of the Afterlife but rather a multitude of Beyonds, like so many dreams made by each soul. Each soul builds its own dwelling place in the same way that it generates 'dreamlike bubbles.'

"Listening to conversations and attending meetings here and there, I have often found that many who believe in the survival of the soul generally believe that once lightened of the weight of the flesh, the soul is immediately absorbed by the Light. They imagine that the consciousness that characterizes a soul expands immediately and enters into a state of understanding and lightness that allows him or her to join a world of beauty, a kind of paradise where they will finally rest. This may be true, since the destination of a soul freed from its earthly obstacles is higher spheres of existence, each one more and more luminous.

"This may be true, but it does not automatically happen. It must be recognized that few of us are completely free

173

from material appetites and, therefore, from some form of enslavement to the density of our world.

"The majority of souls who compose our humanity, even with the best of intentions, still live in a sort of half-light of consciousness. Their choices and priorities are not clearly defined.

It is logical that what a soul lacks in clarity on Earth follows her to the 'Other Side.' Creating her own reality, she spontaneously projects the 'light/dark' of the terrestrial world around her and holds onto it because she can't let go."[32]

Chapter XV

How Do You Envision Your
Own Death and What Comes After?

Testimonies and Reflections

"Is it not written that we must ask to receive? We are the entrance door to an infinity of dwelling places. So why not use our lives to do everything in order to obtain the keys? If we want to liberate ourselves, I think it is first necessary to learn how to distinguish the nature of the bars of our prison."

— Daniel Meurois

Dr. Jean-Jacques Charbonnier
(physician, anesthesiologist, author)

How I envision my own death:

All my research and work on this subject gave me the strength to befriend death and dying. Although I fear pain and physical suffering, I am absolutely not afraid of death. It is part of life and even necessary. To live too long in this same earthly body would be like wanting to dance for years wearing the same increasingly worn-out costume. It must be boring. Moreover, it is the reflection of many people who, once past the threshold of ninety or ninety-five years, say when their lucidity allows it, "It's good now. I lived and lived well. I can go!"

There are many countries where death is not at all sad, where it is even celebrated joyfully because it represents a transition of life and not a final and absolute end. And it is not in these countries that there are more suicides than elsewhere. On the contrary, there are much fewer than in France!

Suicide is the result of a civilization of desperate people who consider death a definitive end rather than a transition. A person will commit suicide thinking that doing so will once and for all eliminate all the problems he or she has. This is not the right solution because these problems will have to be fixed in one way or another in other planes of existence.

Following death on the material plane, one wonders what happens on the spiritual plane. There are those who have experienced clinical death and come back with memories of their singular journeys. These "Guides of the Beyond" give us a lot of indications as to what awaits us on the Other Side of the Veil.

Still, the question remains: What happens next? Do you evolve in other planes? Are you wandering between two worlds, wanting to attach yourself to certain earthly goods or even ignoring your own death? Do you go back to Earth in a new incarnation? I believe that the three latter scenarios are possible.

Regarding reincarnation, some people write to me saying that they do not understand how a medium is able to give information about a deceased person if this person is already reincarnated. This question is very relevant, and I offer the following answer. In the Afterlife, time does not exist. There is not the linear flow that we know on this planet. The future, past, and present merge, or rather do not mean anything anymore. The testimonials of those who've experienced it give us this notion of timelessness with their precognitive and retrocognitive visions.

Quantum physics corroborates this notion by telling us that an event taking place in one reality occurs simultaneously in another reality in a parallel universe. In other words, we can exist simultaneously in several parallel worlds and even at different times. It's quite vertiginous.

In our terrestrial vibration, there are also cases of bilocation, where some awakened people, like Padre Pio, have been observed in several places at the same time. In such an instance, we are observing that psychic connections are not in contradiction with the concept of reincarnation. On our terrestrial plane, these phenomena seem at odds with the single space-time system that we commonly know.

To summarize my response in a succinct way, I envision my death with a lot of serenity. The route that will take my mind will be the one I have studied for thirty years. I will not be too surprised to witness my own death and being cleared of my earthly body, finding a light of love at the end of the dark tunnel, seeing all my life in every detail, and being welcomed by the loved ones who've preceded me, as well as the animals I've loved.

When the Being of Light asks me, "What did you do with your life? How did you help and love others?" I will answer that I did my best, but I could have done better. And then we will decide on a new existence for me: to evolve in the Invisible or to return again to our terrestrial plane. I do not think I'll be a wandering soul, hanging around for a long time in this world. I have studied this way too much to doubt its existence.

For a list of the writings of Dr. Jean-Jacques Charbonnier, published in French, see the end of this book.

Laila Del Monte *(medium-therapist for the animal soul; author; teacher in Spain, France, and North America [Canada and the U.S.])*

When I was a little girl, my parents told me that after death, there was nothing left, just bones and dirt. This notion caused me great anxiety. For me, it was absolutely impossible that there could be nothing after. This idea tortured me, and I thought about it a lot. I could not imagine the ending of my "self." How could my "self" not exist? It was inconceivable! Since then, I have come to understand that this feeling of my "self" is not my personality. It is my consciousness. After having gone through death several times, my life path led me, from childhood until now, to be in contact with "spirit medicine" healers. I am lucky to have been cured by them. I have also been able to encounter Beings of Light of extraordinary kindness and compassion.

After these experiences, I am absolutely certain of the existence of another side, where there is sublime knowledge and love. I'm not afraid of death anymore.

"Why are you crying about what does not die?"

This is what the "doctors of Heaven" told me when I cried with all my might over the loss of my little Siamese cat, who was hit by a car. He was just six months old. He was my angel. His name was Chulo.

It was so unfair! I did not understand why he had to be taken away from me. Even though I knew of the existence of the Afterlife, the pain of the loss was very real and cruel. It was twenty years ago.

Since then, I have been extremely fortunate to have had many experiences and conversations with the "doctors," and I became unafraid of "the After." These years with the "doctors" completely changed my vision of things. I understand that we are here for a short time to learn and be happy, but our real "home" is on the Other Side, where we are never alone. We are accompanied. There, we have the opportunity to learn, evolve, and help others. For me, the earthly dimension and the Other Side exist together daily. There is no difference.

I am not afraid of death, but I am still afraid of dying. I am afraid of disease, of the process of dying, of stopping breathing and letting go of the physical body. I realize that I still have work to do to shed that fear.

178

I'm also scared for those I love—my family and relatives who have not experienced the beauty on the Other Side. I am afraid to see how they manage their departures.

What consoles me and helps me to live is that I know that the doctors and Beings of Light will be there to help me when the day comes.

One day, they told me not to worry about it, that they would pick me up when it's time. And then, another day when I was talking about the distant future, they told me that I would be with them at this time with their group.

So I try to focus daily on the teachings: Be happy, find joy in all things, take care of my health, and do what I love, which is helping animals.

All people have guides and beings around them. If we get in touch with them through prayer and thought, we lose the fear of what is on the Other Side of the Veil. On this Other Side of the Veil, there is so much love! The Other Side of the Veil is infinite.

For a list of the writings of Laila Del Monte, published in French, see the end of this book.

Dr. Eric Dudoit *(PhD in psychology, theologian, author, teacher in the School of Medicine in Aix-en-Provence, hospice practitioner in the Hospital of La Timone in Marseille, founder of the Clinic of Spirit)*

(Marseille, May 15, 2017) The question of how I envision my death and its aftermath reminds me of an article by Mr. de M'Uzan, entitled "IID: If I Was Dead," and the work of another psychoanalyst, D. Anzieu, who each morning read the obituaries in his daily paper, apprehensive that one day he would see his own name. In childhood, we play the game "If I Were Dead" in a kind of bucolic or anxious daydream. This daydream refers us to what R. Otto calls "the fascination and terror" one feels in the face of great questions without existential answers.

Of course, after more than twenty years practicing in a palliative care unit as a psychologist, I have contemplated death. I've even smelled, touched, "tasted," seen, and heard death many times. But knowledge without experience is not knowledge, strictly speaking. Thus, this writing is well on the side of what I envision and imagine.

If given the choice, I would avoid a violent and accidental death. I think my job has influenced the way I would like to die—that is, consciously and with a little bit of time to think about it. Unlike most people I ask, I do not wish to be asleep. Like Ramana Maharshi, I would like this experience to lead a little more toward enlightenment, toward the love of others, to the very heart of this love.

To do this, I think I will need time to give up my personality. He has so cluttered me, this one, in my present life that I would simply like to get rid of him like an old coat, with a smile.

I think I will be afraid of leaving those I love and also this very beautiful planet. This fear of which I speak will not be terror; it will be as soft as the breeze of Elijah while in the desert, the prophet waiting for the coming of the Unnamed.

To return to an accidental death, it leads me to remember the painter Pollock, who said while painting in his "dripping" style, "I deny the accident!" But life led him to a brutal death.

I also remember the day I was unable to catch my breath due to a pneumopathy, and I perfectly remember the emotions I experienced: amazement, stupor followed by fright, then a strange sense of well-being occurring at the same moment as a myriad of lights before my eyes, like a narcosis of the depths. Finally, as if having let go and enabling my lungs to resume their functioning, I started breathing again.

Death seems to me a mystery that humans have to solve in this century. According to some, this will be spiritual, while others think it won't be (a quote unjustly attributed to A. Malraux). As long as death continues to signify destruction in people's minds, we will not be able to free ourselves from the social conditionings influencing the act of dying.

So, unlike many of my Western contemporaries, it's not so much to live forgetting we are going to die that interests me, but to live fully with the presence of death and to enjoy every moment of life.

In fact, would there be a real life without death? This leads me to consider not life in opposition to death but life as comprising moments of life and moments of death. And this naturally invites me to share my faith in life after life.

As you may suspect, I think we have a multitude of "lives," all adorned with a multitude of "deaths." While it is true that most of us do not know everything about our past lives, I still think that one's body has indelible traces of them. The wonderful connection between a body and a soul, both building together toward a loving harmonization, allows the soul to choose a place and a time or multiple places and times to incarnate according to the desired experience.

As far as the "Afterlife" is concerned, my conception is this: At the moment of death, the soul breaks away from the physical body, and what the Ancients called the "silver cord" breaks. This sliver cord is made of an energetic tissue that allows the soul to free itself from the physical body during sleep and/or out-of-body experiences.

Often before death, a person creates a sort of airlock in which he or she can think and find loved ones. This airlock is a parallel universe that functions like a dream according to the awareness of the person dying. The movie *Inception*, with its notion of nested dreams, can give you an idea of what this is like, as can the film *What Dreams May Come*.

The moment of death is, it seems to me, comparable in all respects to the imminent death experiments with different components described by Dr. Greyson and Dr. Moody. These

181

different components (four for Greyson and fifteen for Moody) are all of the same typology described by Professor Kenneth Ring. This psychosociologist has also highlighted in a book the therapeutic benefits of stories of imminent death experiences for individuals afraid of dying.

To summarize these works and my own work, death is seen as a succession of sequences (a tunnel, light, an out-of-body experience, a feeling of infinite love), and what follows is an entrance into worlds just as real and true in a phenomenological sense as ours. The worlds of the Afterlife correspond to different vibratory levels, different states of consciousness testifying to the consciousness of the deceased.

Death, as such, does not mean the end of the ego but rather a new understanding of what the greats of the humanities who've preceded us have called the "self." Thus, my conception of life after life is at the same time in continuity and rupture with this earthly life—a continuity of all the phenomena and sensations experienced in our world but multiplied and a rupture because of the fact that each of our lives has a beginning and an end.

For a list of the writings of Dr. Eric Dudoit, published in French, see the end of this book.

Dr. Guy Londechamp *(doctor, researcher of energy medicine)*

I was born into a family hit hard by unfair and premature deaths, the kinds that leave deep wounds in the descendants.

My father's paternal grandfather died on March 25, fifteen days after my dad was born, and my dad left this world, ninety years later, on March 25 too. How could this be merely a weird coincidence?

At fifteen, he lost his father by suicide. Then at eighteen, his mother died of tuberculosis.

182

His sister, returning after two years of captivity in Nazi Germany, died of tuberculosis as well. For his entire life, he couldn't talk about it without anger and tears.

On my mother's side, it's worse. Her father died violently in prison in Ukraine when she was two years old, and she successively lost her four young brothers aged between six and eighteen years due to poverty, lack of medical care, and war. Later, her father-in-law died when he was in captivity in Germany.

It can be said that I came from violent, painful, and unacceptable circumstances. My maternal grandmother transmitted a great life force to her daughter, and I see her in my children today. I believe she also brought to us a deep sense of anger and opposition to injustice.

This veil left by brutal death—I felt it on me when I was very young. It made me move all the time and practice sometimes dangerous sports, like off-piste skiing, kayaking in very hot water, climbing without protection, and so on. I felt its breath on me many times, almost always while I was in water or snow.

As I grew older, there's no doubt my awareness of my "genealogical fate" moved me to specialize in emergency medicine and hospice care. In medical school, I attended classes during the day and worked nights as a part-time nurse. I wanted to conquer death or delay it as much as possible but also understand its genius, feel its smell.

It took me a long time and many confrontations to realize how powerless I was and to grasp the profound ignorance of the medical studies I completed. There is no room for consciousness in so-called "scientific courses."

However, quantum physics and biophysics have been studied for a century, and transpersonal psychology and studies on near-death experiences (NDEs) have been developed for at least twenty years. And I haven't even mentioned the East Asian, Indian, and Tibetan philosophies and esoteric knowledge dealing with the nature of energy and consciousness, astrology, and the world of senses that some regions around the world have kept alive.

In my medical practice, I learned to feel, to open other worlds of information, to describe the energy and the state of order of a living system. I tried above all to convey meaning and understand the right choices that were accessible to me because of expanded, structured, and hierarchized representations of knowledge.

By collecting scientific research from all sides and doing daily tests during consultations, I came to look at the human body as a liquid hologram—more likely a liquid crystal—driven by fields of consciousness and frequencies totally governed by chemistry and physiology.

From this angle, illness can be seen as a discordance, a partial or general chaos gradually leading to death: the complete "release" of the information gained during life. The biophysicist Fritz-Albert Popp calls it a "swan song," the last and most beautiful song expressed in this world, the signature at the bottom of the book one writes in this level of density in the energy consciousness.

I have helped people with very advanced fatal illnesses who seemed to be cured but then died within three days. Some died the day after receiving treatments! The physical attacks were no longer detectable through scanning or MRIs, but I knew they were still occurring. The body was no longer supporting the work of collecting information!

In fact, this bioluminescence—literally, bright biological essence—comes from your DNA, which is structured by light called "biophotons." All of your cells communicate in the ultraviolet, and it is this permanent exchange of coherent light, of an ultralow laser type, that coordinates your organism and your incarnated consciousness at every moment.

Such radiation can be changed instantly by emotion, thought, food, a cell phone, medicinal drugs, and of course the water we drink or bathe in.

Why water?

The body is made up of 70 percent liquid. The brain is organized around ventricles of cerebrospinal fluid placed at the center of the "sensory transducer" of the consciousness. Your DNA does not work without water. That is to say that the quality of the water completely conditions your consciousness without your knowledge, which I can verify with ten years of continuous tests supported by the fine imaging of Dr. Korotkov's GDV camera.[33]

In your DNA, 3 percent of the genes is enough to operate the biology of the body, while the remaining 97 percent of semicrystalline genes (long, repetitive sequences that do not code for protein synthesis) have historically been considered "waste genes" by rational biologists before being very recently looked at by Professor Chang as a second code. This second code is probably of alien origin mixed with terrestrial genes for the evolution of species on Earth. There is also a possibility of a connection to the Akashic Field, or "memory of the universe," of Ervin Laszlo.

The famous mathematician Emile Pinel, father of the theory of cell fields and chronobiology, explained that time does not exist in a person's cell nuclei (DNA), and upon physical death, the component H1, which connects you to the terrestrial magnetic field, vanishes, leaving the psychobiological H3 component to merge with the H2 component of memory (the Akashic Field). This merging persists "for a certain time" after death, and there is no way to calculate the length of the duration because of the change of coordinates.... For me, death reveals the true nature of consciousness within the universe and its origins.

In this period of my life, in active retirement, I believe I no longer fight against death. Rather, I intend to increase my coherence and the luminous order that it generates, to offer to the world around me and also very far from me the fruit of my life, which is understanding and experiencing, with some wisdom gained through given treatments as a doctor and suffering I encountered in my patients.

Going back to the source is like becoming living water, flowing and rebounding off of the reefs of life by absorbing a greater light from the explosion of water drops[34]—from people dying and beautifully letting go, giving everything back to the world. This swan song invitation encourages me to be ready for death at any time and at the same time welcome all of what life is about.

The worlds my consciousness will be "attracted" to later will be those I have believed in and nourished or created here below; hence, there is this deep need for simplicity and fluidity—silence too. This is where I can best feel gratitude and love for life.

For a list of the writings of Dr. Guy Londechamp, published in French, see the end of this book.

Mark Vallée
(editor and founder of Ariane Editions, author, lecturer)

My Death and After

I've read books on the astral journey for the last twenty years. I found a very interesting book about the Afterlife, *Life in the World Unseen*, written by the medium Anthony Borgia, who transcribed the thoughts of a deceased English Anglican priest, Robert Hugh Benson, about communicating with the spirit world and his experience of the passage from death to the subtler planes of life, a passage that awaits each of us upon death. There was a very intriguing description of these planes or dimensions of life as something that evolves according to the awakening of consciousness of the individual. Each plane has its own frequency and its own reality, and at death, you find yourself in a place automatically matching your frequency.

Over the years, several books have served to fine-tune my knowledge on the subject. For example, I liked the books of author Michael Roads, who had the ability to consciously project himself onto these planes, indicating that it was not

186

necessary to wait for death to access other realities. Life was then revealed in its multidimensional aspects and became more and more fascinating because, of course, its dimensions are inhabited by different forms of life and we are called to meet them.

Thanks to these interests, this passion, I discovered throughout my life information that not only soothed me about what awaits at death but also gave me the motivation to work on myself daily while here on this earthly plane. This kind of information, combined with a rather natural belief in these notions, made sense and convinced me that the Afterlife is real.

Still, my approach remained theoretical. It was upon the death of my mother, which occurred in 2011, that I had an experience directly relating to this Afterlife. During a lucid dream, I saw my mother. It was about six months after she died. She had come to say goodbye. I think she was accessing a plane further away from our terrestrial plane. This goodbye was, above all, a sharing of love, a love that only such a plane of existence enables one to sense and give. So I was bathed in love, a simple and pure love that marks you for life.

I later had contact with another deceased member of my family—my sister, who died in 2015. Again, about six months after her death, when I was experiencing significant stress, she came to tell me in a lucid dream that my worry was useless and unconstructive. I already knew this, but hearing it and feeling it—because in this dimension, "feeling" is very alive—changed the situation. Such feeling has a powerful impact on reshaping one's reality. I had found a solid anchor and, of course, experienced the joy of seeing my sister, whom I'd been very close to.

For me, death will be a return home after having lived an incarnation mandate. I was told that I had experienced a difficult past. Despite the obstacles of the present, my life is full of joy and harmony, not pain. A life that makes sense is a life where happiness is present.

We are multidimensional beings, and the earth plane is only one of our possible "playgrounds."

I am convinced that one day we will be able to come to Earth to live experiences, and we will not be blocked or limited by dimensional parameters. We will be able to leave at will to go to another planet or another plane of life of our choosing. I can't wait for this day!

For a list of the writings of Mark Vallée, published in French, see the end of this book.

Annie Lautner *(author, poet)*

(March 14, 2017) I was confronted by death early in life. As a result of the circumstances of my birth, I had to fight for three and a half months against an illness that forced me to be hospitalized and separated from my family, who only saw me once a week through a window.

I recovered, and since then, the topic of death has never left me.

Following the deaths of my paternal grandparents, my father's pain was such that I promised myself I would find the answers to my questions because, for me, death could not be summed up by this grief. I was fifteen years old.

Subsequently, throughout my life's journey, I have come across readings and had encounters that, little by little, confirmed to me the idea that death is simply a passage from one state to another.

I have always intuitively believed in a life after death, and my spiritual quest has strengthened my belief in this. I bathe today in this quietude of being that connects me to all that lives. Around the age of thirty, a friend introduced me to the works of Daniel Meurois, and upon reading them, there was no longer any doubt.

As a hospice counselor, I have guided many terminally ill and aging patients at the end of life. These have been intense moments for me, and full of love. My approach is to be present, listening and giving the best of myself to allow those who die to leave serenely.

Regarding my own departure, I am totally at peace, and I have already informed my children that I do not wish to have any medical interventions. Just let me go when the time is right.

Do not forget that a death here is a birth beyond. Respecting this sacred moment is extremely important to me. Do not hold back the one who is leaving; rather, give him or her all your love, which will be the only luggage at the moment of passage.

As far as my "after," I can only see it brightly and in continuity with my earthly mission: to give love and to awaken consciences to the Paths of Light.

For a list of the writings of Annie Lautner, published in French, see the end of this book.

Johanne Razanamahay *(shaman, author, teacher)*

Originally from Madagascar, I am a shaman-medium. I see all kinds of subtle realities. I have been in contact since my childhood with various spiritual entities that inspire and guide me in shamanic journeys. They train me to leave my physical body and enter into pure consciousness.

I know the processes of life and death. Seeing for so long those who arrive on Earth and those who depart for the Other Side of the Veil, I am familiar with the phenomena. As a result, I am no longer impressed by anything. Better still, I am increasingly enchanted when I meet all kinds of beings that are manifested to me in various forms, expressing themselves in a thousand ways. When one is not anchored well in his or her core, this is not obvious.

Death is one of the least understood phenomena in modern society, even though it is simply another spiritual adventure.

When we are not educated to perceive its meaning, death can seem absurd and unacceptable, even to me. I spontaneously live in extraordinary and incredible parallel worlds, but I had to experience many of these fantastic phenomena, meet many amazing beings, and observe many deceased persons, including family members, to discern the reason for being and the spiritual goal of death.

My Malagasy origin kept me from revolting against the death of the physical body because of my acceptance of the truthfulness of the experiences in the nonmaterial worlds. In Madagascar, we believe in life after death, and a whole cult exists to honor ancestors and dialogue with them.

Today, in my opinion, the phenomenon of Passage to the Afterlife is just as important as birth on Earth and should not be dismissed. As death is only a bridge from one world to another, for those who are nearing the end of their time on Earth or no longer have the courage to continue their experiences, life could be better lived by not avoiding death.

If we make an effort to find out what is happening and being said in many parts of our world about the process of dying, then we can accompany people positively and serenely. We can do this if our deepest desire is truly to see people shine with happiness and peace, both in their earthly existence and after death.

To achieve this, the first thing is to open a big chapter on the meaning and value of existence so that all of us can move toward spiritual realization. Then each of us will be able to die quietly when it is time.

We are currently still living in confusion by scattering ourselves in all directions. As a result, we do not really enjoy life, and we die badly, even running the risk of becoming "wandering souls" because we are too ignorant of how to go to the kingdoms of Heaven.

190

Only the physical body can die. One's consciousness never dies, nor do the subtle bodies that are connected to it. What I reveal here is not a personal belief but a reality recognized by millions of people from the beginning of life on Earth. Without ever knowing or meeting each other, human beings who have lived separated by huge oceans or very high mountains have told all the same stories.

My dream is to die free, without having to endure the burdens of the state, medicine, religion, or family. We could allow people to die peacefully in nature, in beautiful places, without burial, as the elephants do, for example. There are already some cultures where people are withdrawing from their families to die alone.

I will add to my wishes the possibility of having the choice to avoid medical interventions that keep me alive when I cannot do anything other than remain stuck in a bed, enriching the medical system to the detriment of my family. I would also like to note that a body saturated with chemistry is a body that is indigestible to the earth, and it pollutes the food of all living beings!

Finally, my dearest wish is for my family to not pay for the manufacture of a tomb or coffin in concrete or steel with a cross or epitaph on it. I think that's a great comedy and a big lie. Why? Because my body will be more accessible to the life force that needs it for the continuity of living beings of all realms if it is not put in a concrete or steel box.

As I enjoy life more and more, I am preparing myself for a peaceful and happy death and a welcoming by enchanting beings who sing of my identity in the fantastic realms. In the rainbow colors, I will breathe in plenitude before jumping happily from one plane to another, creating all sorts of wonders dreamed of and benefiting from the creations of all those who radiate while living in this infinite happiness. I will always live connected with my people and all living beings!

In the meantime, I serve others in various ways, either alone or with my family and committed friends. All those who contact me should know that I am ready to use my gifts and talents to help them attain greater awareness so they can live healthfully and die peacefully.

For a list of the writings of Johanne Razanamahay, published in French, see the end of this book.

Chantal Dejean *(lecturer on the subject of death, practitioner of the Essenian and Egyptian therapies [Italy and France])*

I still remember the day I awoke with a start in my bed. I was a teenager. I felt like I was being invaded by despair and anguish. A reality outside of mine was condensing around me, and someone was shouting for help. A familiar silhouette began to take shape at the foot of my bed. I very quickly recognized his features, his brown hair and blue eyes. An uncle I loved very much was standing right in front of me.

With my medium abilities, I'd already had several experiences that allowed me to get in touch with other facets of life, but this was different. This uncle did not belong to these other realities, so why was I having these sensations and this vision?

Shortly after my panicked wake-up, my phone rang, and I was told that the uncle in question had just killed himself. This was the beginning of my passages from the gate of the world of the dead ones. The bond of love that had united me with my uncle since my childhood helped me to accompany him step by step on his journey in the Afterlife. Afterward, I was able to help other beings who, like him, found themselves helpless after death.

Following several years of accompaniments and meetings with the deceased, I learned to consider any form of life an energy that vibrates at a different frequency than ours.

One's consciousness can come into contact with these different forms of life by being in tune with their vibrations, accepting that there are other "vibratory ranges" in addition to ours.

Death is therefore for me a simple change of a channel that allows you to strip your soul of its earthly dimension to find its original state, that of being a spark of the Divine.

Without a doubt, death can be difficult or painful for those who leave as well as for those who remain, but we must welcome love every day within us and open up to our true selves, integrating our multidimensionality with that of LIFE, where death no longer exists. We will then finally understand that the Passage is only one more door to a multitude of facets of life.

Marie-Chantal Martineau *(author, artist-illustrator, medium-therapist, teacher of the Angelic Tianshi therapies)*

How do I envision my death? What a great and inevitable question! Death has haunted my mind since I was very young. As a teenager, the loss of loved ones led me to reflect on this question, and the writing of my next book has thrown me once more into the heart of this mystery.

When I was a little girl, around the age of five or six, a Petula Clark song was played regularly on the radio ("Everyone Wants to Go to Heaven, But No One Wants to Die"). During the first notes, I'd automatically stop my playing. Whenever I heard the song, I went into a kind of daydream and imagined what Heaven might be like.

The lyrics of the song still resonate with me: "I would like to be an angel and then live in paradise. There, everyone is happy. It is always a nice day...." The lyrics did not explain everything to me, though, and I remained confused and worried.

I did not know then that I would need a lifetime to find some understanding of this phenomenon, some nuggets of light drawn here and there from my readings, my mystical experiences, and the hollow of my soul.

I realized that my soul, my immortal self, will remain after the last beat of my heart. Just as I did in the nocturnal astral trips of my childhood, I will fly to another world, to a new home. I will go home!

I have always sensed that my physical heart will answer the call of my soul when it is ready to fly. As I have an irregular heartbeat, it is natural for me to think that it will be through my heart that I will be liberated from my physical body.

But when? Who can tell? I can see the number eighty, and maybe a few more years. I don't know. I imagine that I will fly gently, during my sleep perhaps, like slipping into my dreamworld at night, or very slowly, in the hospital, without any fear. At last, I'll wish it. I know that death is nothing more than a transformation. I will leave my cocoon of flesh to deploy my beautiful butterfly wings, surrounded by my loved ones, children, and grandchildren holding my hand. At least, I hope so.

My heart may have offered its last beat on Earth, but its magic will accompany me in another way. It will beat again, but much more subtly. My Body of Light will be as weightless as the breath of an angel, and I will smile.

I will refind my youth, and I will certainly have a radiant face. In fact, I will have the appearance I had on Earth, but brighter. I will find the Divine Love within me and feel an incredible sense of well-being, something I experienced in a dream once when I was young. I still remember what it was like. I will find this Divine Love in me, and it will guide me like an interior lighthouse and raise me up so I can cross the tunnel that separates the worlds.

The light at the end of this tunnel will melt in my soul, and I will see coming toward me my dear love, my terrestrial husband, surely gone before me. Our reunion will be wonderful, and my happiness in joining him will be immense. I will dive again into the infinity ocean of his blue eyes, and we will embrace each other tenderly.

At his side will be my dear parents, my terrestrial father and mother. With great happiness, I will find them. Their kindly smiles and open arms will fill me with joy. I will also find all those I lost throughout my life. They will come to welcome me. I will also find relatives who remained on the other planes during my earthly odyssey. And, with much happiness, I will thank those who have guided my steps—my angels and guides who, at my side, accompany me on my way.

I will have so much to discover. Divine Love will illuminate my soul, and I will be led to a great celebration of reunion in my new city and my new home. I will discover these new places with joy and hope. My house will be like the one I had on Earth but brighter and more radiant. Its luxuriant nature will delight me. My home will be surrounded by multicolored flowers, majestic and vibrant trees, clear lakes, and singing waterfalls. My little white dogs, so loved on Earth, will join me, free and happy.

I will then review my earthly life, feeling all the emotions of love and pain, both mine and those of others, because my soul will melt into the souls of others. I will be proud of the challenges overcome. When guilt invades my soul in the face of lack of love and mistakes made in my life journey, I will hear in the center of my being words of comfort and love pronounced telepathically by my angels and guides. These words will comfort my heart and confirm that the Divine Love that lives in me will help me forgive myself.

I will also visit the Celestial Library with the soul of my dear love, my husband on Earth. I will be proud to discover with him the celestial versions of our books, those we wrote and those we edited. We will discover the good that our work brought to the earth. We will hold hands, happy.

I know I will have a lot to do and offer.

My earthly experience as an adoptive mother may allow me to help babies and children who left before their parents did. Or, perhaps my work in energy therapy will resume. It may also be through painting or writing that I will again offer my help and my light. And why not continue our common mission? My husband and I will begin sharing knowledge again, this time in celestial workshops!

Who knows what the next part of my story will be! But what I do know is that my mission of love started on Earth will continue in the Beyond. Yes, I will continue to love.

For a list of the writings of Marie-Chantal Martineau, published in French, see the end of this book.

Alain Williamson *(founder and CEO of Éditions Le Dauphin Blanc, editor, author, trainer, translator)*

Love never dies.

I have always reflected on death, from the pews of church when I was a child to the fullness of my maturity. Paradoxically, I have a huge desire to live. Although this terrestrial world is imperfect and chaotic, I am happy to live here and play a role, as modest as it is. But I have always been aware that I will have to leave this world someday. Life gave me breath at birth, and I will have to return it to him one day or another.

How will this departure unfold? I do not know. Will death take me by surprise, in the wake of an accident or heart attack? Or will he visit me during long months of illness, patient like a spider at the bottom of her web?

I wish I could die very slowly, like an old car running out of fuel. I would like to die naturally, in full awareness of the passage to be undertaken. Though this expression may seem strange, I want to die fully alive, surrounded by the love of those dear to me. This is the vision that I maintain, the one I see.

With my penchant for melancholy and nostalgia, I will probably be saddened to no longer be able to hug my sweetheart and my children.

And then, there is still this physical body programmed for survival. Will it resist? Maybe. It is up to me to let go, to cast it off and move on to my soul body. I will leave people I love, but I will find others too. In one dimension, we will cry about my departure; in another, we will celebrate my arrival. Birth and death are to life what inhaling and exhaling are to breathing—two events in the same movement.

I like to think that leaving my earthly life will be like leaving the office and going home after a busy day of work. In this sense, Jesus' words serve as a beacon for me: "I am in this world, but not of this world." In recent years, this is the vision that I have wanted to develop. I am a soul on a mission, just as each soul is by the way. I will complete this mission, and then I will return to my home.

And what will it be like at home? I see it as beautiful, bright, and warm. I love the sea and its infinite horizons, and I imagine there will be a similar decor. I see it as a place of rest and relaxation. At least, that's probably what I'll need in the early days of my return. I see myself free, surrounded by nature and fully in my essence. And I will be nurtured by peace, the peace that is sorely lacking on Earth.

There will probably be a review that needs to be done of my most recent incarnation. And I will remember that guilt is bad and useless. There is love, only love. I will have, I hope, the feeling of having accomplished something good, of having walked toward my true nature. There were some missteps, of course, but overall the evolutionary leaps on my spiritual journey will prevail. No doubt I will be aware that I could have loved even more, lived even more, as love requires. And that will possibly tinker with my next incarnation destination.

I will continue to explore creativity and the infinite worlds of love, admire creation, deepen my understanding of the divine mystery, and share with the souls I love. The sceneries will change, the states will be modified, but the bonds of love will remain. I like to think that my wife, my children, my parents, my friends, and my dogs—all my bonds of love—will exist beyond the terrestrial plane. Deep down, love is at the heart of each of these relationships, and that love never dies.

After my death, I will continue to live! Even more intensely! I now know where my immense desire to live comes from: eternity.

For a list of the writings of Alain Williamson, published in French, see the end of this book.

Hélène Giroux *(author, end-of-life coach)*

How do I envision my death and what comes after?

This is a question we rarely hear discussed in conversations. Many things evolve at a pace sometimes difficult to follow over the years, but our understanding of death—this step that is a part of each person's path—remains murky and continues to frighten many people.

Death has been on my mind the last few years, and I think of it more and more because I believe it is the goal of incarnation. You come to fulfill your mission in life, bring your humble share and uniqueness to this world, and then return home. I am not so different from the majority of people I meet, but the vocation I chose, that of spending time with people preparing to cross to the Other Side of the Veil, has led me to be regularly confronted with the question of death and to think about it while with these beings who experience it concretely. I think about it every time I find myself at the bedside of a dying person, because this thinking evolves at the same rate that I evolve as a human.

This question is so important! If I had been asked it fifteen or twenty years ago, I humbly admit that my answer would have been very different. In fact, I don't think I would have spent a long time thinking about it. Like the majority of people, death was rarely discussed in my life unless we were confronted by the loss of a loved one.

I have been working with end-of-life people for over ten years now, and my ideas have really changed from being with these people I consider to be teachers. Most of those I talk to want a quick death while sleeping. I personally would prefer to have time to settle my affairs, take stock of my passage on Earth, talk to my relatives, ask forgiveness from people, and say I love you.

I would like to consciously die. This wish may seem strange to some, but I know it is possible because I've had the immense privilege of observing it with several people—more, indeed, than might be expected. I confess honestly that I find this notion fascinating!

Addressing this question brings me back to the birth of my first son. I am frequently making connections between birth and death because I believe there are so many. At that time, I was young and scared, but I was also deeply certain I was having a great experience that would change my life, beyond the suffering, pain, and fear I felt. So I chose to consciously live through the experience without using anything to numb the pain or speed up the process. When, after thirteen hours of labor, the doctor began to talk about the possibility of a C-section, I felt strongly that this was not how things would happen. I ended up having my son naturally, and I was not mistaken about the experience in the end. It was spectacular!

I believe in the order of things and the experiences that cross my path, and I also believe that all of this was orchestrated by my soul before my arrival in this world. I trust that she brings me to where I should be, and everything serves my evolution.

At the moment when my soul feels it is time to go, I see myself remaining lucid until the very end because I believe that this moment will be a great experience and that you continue to learn and evolve until the last breath.

I am not saying that I will be free from fear, because it is still an unknown experience. I hope, though, that the learning I've taken part in during my earthly journey will give me the tools I need to cross the Passage with serenity.

I see myself also surrounded by people who have been important to me, and I will be filled with a sense of happiness due to the long and fruitful journey of my life. Preparing for this moment is actually like preparing for a trip. This is done in stages, and each one has a meaning, a reason for being. The best way for me to prepare for such a trip is to live my life consciously as often as possible. It is not only at the end when you should dwell on it. There are opportunities every day. I really believe that, on the Other Side, I will find people I have loved and known, and with all the people I've encountered, there will be so many! It will be a joy to see them again, and I will feel free and lighter. I will welcome this new experience with curiosity!

This will also be the moment to look back at all the progress I made and what I understood and assimilated from this incarnation. I am expecting to evaluate my contribution to this world because I deeply believe that our role is to sow love through our acts and words.

I will also see my guides and all the Beings of Light who accompanied me throughout my life journey and from whom I have so often asked for assistance. I will explore this other dimension like a child marveling at a new world. And, to be honest, my work over the years with end-of-life people has nearly given me a reason to be excited to die.

For a list of the writings of Hélène Giroux, published in French, see the end of this book.

200

Dr. Mark Medvesek *(doctor and therapist, Reunion Island; practitioner of humanitarian medicine, Madagascar)*

How I envision my death:

To be honest, I have always been interested in the mystery of death as well as the mystery of the cosmos that surround us. As far back as I can remember, I've sought to understand the meaning of my life. I searched and searched, eventually finding myself in agreement with my consciousness, a vision of the meaning of life and a sense of death. It seems obvious to repeat here the words of Heraclitus from 363 BC: "Every death is a birth to another form and every birth, the death of a previous form."

A life flows between these two poles, birth and death, like yin and yang, evolving in the constant pursuit of "becoming." The notion of the "end of life" is meaningless, since it is only a transition on a path. It is a reassuring notion that removes many fears and inertia, enabling one to put life events into perspective.

However, relativizing one's own death does not mean denying it. Regularly confronted with death by the very nature of my job as a doctor, I am surprised to see how disease is such a source of fear—fear of fever, fear of pain, fear of dying.

The role of a doctor is to push this moment back as much as possible. In most cases, people die suddenly, and we do not hear about the deceased after a few days. Even when a person leaves his fingerprints, these always fade with time. No one escapes death.

Death is often portrayed like the sword of Damocles—that is, constantly present, from one's first breath to the last. Should we be afraid of it? Each person will find his or her own answers. For me, it seems more and more obvious that death must be prepared for every second. How? By living life fully and by continually dedicating ourselves to this each day, thereby expanding the limitations of what can be experienced.

Why? Because otherwise, nothing would ripen, and nothing would be able to die. "You do not die of what you are sick, but of what you are alive," Montaigne said.

Sophie Andrieu *(president of Women in Action, pioneer of humanitarian aid, channeling medium, author)*

The Successful Quest for the Best of Oneself
You asked me how I envision my death and what comes after. On a whim! I will certainly have accomplished my soul mission without regret and without embarrassment. Others will have left before me, and I have learned from them. I've always said, "The older you are, the more you know." To gain this knowledge, I drew on the awareness of my older friends!

My work has informed me of the details of preparing for death in all the ancestral traditions of the world, and I will probably choose none. I want death in all its authenticity. I wish to experience the true version of death and face her naked.

The partner I will miss most is my body, which I love and hate. Curiously, it is my body that I think of. I hope not to have hurt it and to be able to offer a healthy body to the belly of my planet, Earth!

It will be one evening in November, the month of my birth. There will be candles. My old, wrinkled hands, joined together, will touch my chest, feeling the life delicately circulating in my body. This will give me a last bit of strength to express my gratitude for my time here.

To fill me one last time with all the emotions available, a little wind will pass through the window and make my flesh tingle, which will signal to me that it's a good night to die. The wear of the soul will be felt. A certain panic will set in to try to move me. It will be the instinct of survival rearing its head.

I am confident the wind will inform me that the sap will stop flowing. At least, that's how I imagine it will be.

I will know then that it's time. I will feel my body touched by the hands of my children. Their presence is the most I could wish for before my departure. My eyes will find those of my husband in his photo beside my bed. He is telling me that all is well. I will take another moment to remember the madness of life, my crazy life!

I will no longer have the strength to remember everything. Where are the flashes of memories? That is definitely designed for those who regret life! I have no regrets. I played all the roles of my life. I disguised myself in all trades. I lived with passion and all my emotions. I had a dream, and I lived my life.

My son holds back tears. He is a powerful man. His fiancée behind the door reassures me of their delicate love. My daughter is furious, but her anger will result in her greatest lesson. Her creativity jostles and amazes me, and I know her brother will be there for her.

I am leaving my physical body with my last breath, though it is not yet time for the great Passage. By transitioning into my Body of Light, I feel I am tilted as an invisible hand stops the beating of my heart. I see all the internal mechanics of my physical body shutting down due to old age. My crumpled thymus gland dries out and contorts itself, life leaving from the last living cell. My silver cord gives way from my physical body in a final clap. I fall into the dark like a light being turned off, but I still feel my blood moving in slow motion. My dying organs send their regards to each other, while my skin remains in survival mode. I am peacefully happy to be an old soul who gave to the earth much more than I took from her!

I then step into the Other Side of the Veil. Elevators run from top to bottom. It makes you dizzy. The tunnel is "overbooked." Everything is going very fast. I understand that it is urgent. I meet so many souls going in the opposite direction!

Wow—everyone is trying to reincarnate. What is happening on Earth?

I meet my forever friend. "Hey, I'm coming. Wait for me!" he tells me. "Namaya (my soul name), I am going down to Earth!"

I just have time to tell him, "But you hated your life on Earth! You had two cancers, an autoimmune disease, your nightmares, your injuries. You wrote fifteen bestselling books!"

He answers, "Namaya, here, it's hell. Believe me, Heaven is on Earth!" He jumps into another elevator and says, "Read and love with the time you have: eternity."

The elevator I'm in stops and opens onto a bright world. I discover my young hands and my heart of twenty years! I sense a rejuvenated tone of voice within me, and I read:

I am experiencing death when I don't pursue my dreams, when I create more obstacles than rewards. I am experiencing death when I feel I am not worthy of embracing all of life's experiences, when I compare and judge people. So I become only compromises to you. I am the sage who slept because your hell burned me. So I leave you, the most hurtful part of me that humiliates my humility, exasperates others, and keeps me in suspense.

I was looking for my truth for a long time before succumbing to diseases. From Heaven, where I am buried, I can tell you that everything is admirable, even my mistakes and especially my differences. I was the height of politeness, the blueprint of good living.

From here, from my death, I can tell you that everything is missing—my desires, my doubts, my chains. When I was down on Earth, I hid them and was ashamed. Well, here I escape all those misfortunes that plundered my time. I am waiting for the ultimate Passage. For the moment, I am in the in-between worlds. I am uncomfortable because I am aware of all that I could be doing alive. So sometimes I get angry, but because I am disembodied, I cannot express it. I still want to feel the sobs that flow in me, feel my eyes swollen by an immense sorrow! Here I am alone, at the doors of the great purification. Confessions and great judgments do not exist. It's worse. You are the master of this grand ceremony. It is you taking an avalanche of judgment, hardness, and separation, all of what you repressed.

Hell is a narrow channel where you judge your life against the paths you chose. Physical death is agile, but psychic death is hellish. It turns into revealing all your exaggerations and dependencies by ignoring the abuses and focusing only on the consequences. It is as though all you learned on Earth was swept away, and what remains are the painful events, not the understanding of the life lessons.

Live your wounds. Do not attempt healing. That is invented to nourish the quest for the best of the self. There is no more mystery here. Dealing with repetitive dysfunctional patterns is a business for those who know that basically nothing will change.

So I tell you, everything changes for the one who speaks to the stars and learns that Fibonacci is a curve that turns only on the self! I am angry because all I have taught is injustice and loss of value. I've assigned so many people to be what they are not. Because we are all messages. Yesterday, I saw a young terrorist come into the Light, so you see, we are all entitled to another life, another chance. For me, soon, I will take the road of reincarnation. Go for yourself. Go for me. Go for my soul, for my personality, for I know that light, too, is bathed in the splendor of life.

I press the button to join the Light that finally doesn't dazzle me anymore. I understand that a new life begins, that of the Divine Self. From my alchemical earthly destiny, I am going to a new world. A strange breath dissolves the self and gathers me in the beautiful center of the Great All! I live in others. I navigate in a frequency that is named here the Divine. It is the single idea of the soul: to be at your best in life!

For a list of the writings of Sophie Andrieu, published in French, see the end of this book.

Daniela Muggia *(editor, Edizioni Amrita, Italy; teacher of end-of-life coaching; speaker; author)*

My Death and What Comes After
Well, I do not consider it. I am one of the people who remembers it. And in my case, it's a troublesome memory.

I was only three or four years old.

I still remember the little red shoes I cared about a lot. I see my little feet walking in a train station. That's where my memory begins.

I know today that it was in a country in Eastern Europe during the winter. I'm wearing a coat, and my father grips my hand. We are running away, and we want to get on a train. I know today that it was during the Second World War. Men in uniform arrive. They scream at us, and they tear me from my father's hand.

End of the First Sequence
The next sequence is in a train full of people. There are no seats. It is a wagon for cattle. I only see legs.

The third sequence is in a concentration camp. I see letters that make up a name, but as I don't know how to read yet, it tells me nothing. Again, I see fear and legs. This time, women's legs.

The fourth sequence is in a closed room with many women. What I don't know is this room is a gas chamber. I now know this. I am in this gas chamber, very small and furious. The women I have been locked up with are very scared, and I cannot do anything for them or for myself. Children often feel responsible for what is happening with adults, and the little one I am is no exception. I feel great fear and, at the same time, immense helplessness and intense hatred for those who did this to us. I do not know what it is, but I am full of terror, despair, and horror. Like all children, I am very empathetic, so I take on the feelings of others.

The next sequence appearing is an after-life memory. I am conscious in an immensity as black and infinite as the night sky. I am not aware of my body, only my Body of Light. I have just the knowledge of something I perceive as "other" that moves forward and will swallow me eventually. It is the egregore[35] of all thoughts of hate, intolerance, and racism since the beginning of the universe. I am distraught, but nothing helps. Now, I am submerged.

I am grateful that my memories stop here. I can tell you today that I know what hell is, and not only hell on earth. Hell is a state of consciousness. You emerge from death according to the state in which you die. *If you die in peace as opposed to hatred and fear, that will make the difference.*

Time does not exist in this hell. It is perhaps in this sense that one speaks sometimes of hell as "eternal." I imagine that something or someone came to extract me, since I'm here today. All of this is to tell you that the *quality* of death is not a subject to be taken lightly. It determines what happens next and, in my experience, can affect even what happens in the next life.

I have long suffered the consequences of all these past events. As a child, I could not play hide-and-seek. The tension was unbearable. I had panic attacks in dark places (in the fifties, being locked in a closet was sometimes a punishment for a child) or with many people, like in a packed elevator. I was afraid of the shower, and I hated uniforms. Later, when I was traveling with my daughter in India, I was scared in the Indian train stations, which are always packed with people. I felt I might "lose it." I constantly saw *the image of an adult hand letting go of a child's hand.*

It was about forty days after my first end-of-life accompaniment, the death of my father, that all these memories flared up.

It was 1991, at the beginning of the war in the former Yugoslavia, and Italian television was showing images of evacuated women landing in an Italian port with Mozart's Requiem playing in the background.

They were very dignified and infinitely sad, often elderly, almost all holding hands with children. And there, suddenly, I was extremely affected. I did not understand why this deep pain had hit me. I had a feeling of suffocation, along with a cold sweat and nausea. I tried to meditate to calm myself down. That, however, opened the door to memories. "Memory" is not the right word, though, because one does not merely "remember." You live it again. And I relived it all. I saw the reality of my room in my present life and at the same time the scene of the train station and the other sequences I described earlier. My mouth was wide open, but I didn't scream. My scream only rang out in the past of my childhood. Everyone tells us that we are going to die as we have lived, but I know that the opposite is true too. *The state in which you die determines how you will live in the Afterlife and even your future lives.*

I imagine that the four-year-old child I was had no time to do any harm, and the way she lived had nothing to do with her terrible death. I can only assume that she was born with a very heavy karma, though that does not justify what happened to her and so many other people. I know she lived her end with great anger and that indeed this egregore was her hell.

So as for my "after"? I do not consider it. I've built it for years. I exercise. I am preparing myself.

Will I be able to leave my body peacefully and let go of the illusion of duality? Can I be totally detached and also united with the universe, moving away from my "personality" and the idea of myself as the subject/object of this world? Will I be free from thoughts of attachment or aversion during my departure?

Will I be able to keep my mind anchored in unconditional compassion? I saw it in action at the end of a life, this compassion excluding nothing and no one.

In this life, my father was Jewish. Having survived the persecution, he finally had a compassionate thought for Hitler, describing him as "the most ignorant man I have ever met in my life." My father had left behind the common dual vision of "good/bad" and instead embraced unconditional compassion, where one is more or less "conscious/ignorant" of the true nature of the soul.

Finally, will I be able to let this body and my ordinary consciousness go to be transferred to the nonlocal consciousness, our true nature? For beyond its most well-known and ordinary aspect, beyond the mind, which the conscience ordinarily uses, it is not local. I know this from *experience*.

In the last few decades, research conducted by outstanding scientists to locate consciousness has yielded nothing, and science's vision of the relationship between the brain and consciousness is far from being unanimously accepted nowadays.

If the reductionist and materialistic hypothesis of many scientists were true—that is, if consciousness were really only a product of the brain—there could be no consciousness during deep sleep, under anesthesia, and even during a clinical death due to cardiac arrest, not to mention memories between two lives. But personal testimonies as well as the studies on NDEs[36] (the so-called "imminent death" experiences that occur during clinical deaths) are here to tell us that when all cerebral activity has ceased, consciousness still exists.

"The absence of explanations to bridge the distance between the brain and consciousness" reminds me of the work of Dr. Pim van Lommel, author of a remarkable study on NDEs[37], *"and the fact that a neural state is certainly not a state of consciousness. We cannot objectify the subjective state of consciousness that is not visible, tangible, perceptible, measurable, verifiable, or "falsifiable.""* So scientific

materialism, which is based only on what is observable, cannot explain what is happening at the level of consciousness, nor the causes or contents of NDEs, such as a hyperacute consciousness perceiving what is happening from an external position above his lifeless body.

Quantum physics helps us. Consciousness, unable to be localized in a given time or space, originates from a nonlocal dimension in the form of waves or information fields (the quantum field is defined as an information field), and a person's brain is none other than the "station" at which these waves or fields of information are received in the form of conscious awareness. Your neural networks operate as interfaces, as transmitters/receivers, not as devices for the storage of consciousness and memories.

The aspect of consciousness that is measurable through neuroimaging techniques such as EEG, fMRI, and PET scans can, while not having its origin in the measurable field of physics, be measured by the collapse of a wave. The interaction between nonlocal consciousness and the material body is a bit like what happens in the field of communications. We are now inundated and traversed by billions of electromagnetic fields due to calls from our cell phones, as well as the presence of TV, radio broadcasts, and websites that can be picked up worldwide. But it's only when we turn on a cell phone, a computer, a radio, or a TV that we become aware of it.

There is no need to browse for this information on the internet. Your laptop does not provide it for you. In the same way, the brain does not produce consciousness. It simply facilitates the experience.

So when you die, it is the body that dies with gradual transformations, of which the Tibetan "science of dying" informs us in a very detailed way. There is also ordinary consciousness or conscious awareness. The electroencephalograph and electrocardiograph display flat lines. As long as you identify with your body and this ordinary consciousness, you will be very afraid of death. This goes without saying, since both have an end.

Only by understanding that we are a part of nonlocal consciousness (and it's unlimited, because it is not linked to space and has no beginning or end, since it is not related to time either) can the fear of death begin to dissolve. However, it is necessary to go beyond mere intellectual comprehension if one wants to succeed at the time of one's death in uniting with the nonlocal consciousness. You must have experienced it and recognized it and learned to stay in it. I love a definition I once heard from the Dalai Lama: *"In this passage, the consciousness passes from the drop level to the ocean level. It is finally promoted!"*

Below are the stages on the path to embracing nonlocal consciousness:

- Experiencing the nonlocal consciousness through meditative states
- Learning how to recognize it
- Having access to it
- And, finally, remaining in it.

Another important teaching: *"If the one who accompanies the dying person enters this state of consciousness through his or her own training, the dying person, who is strongly empathic, can sense this and will be able to stay there more easily. If you want a dying person to die in peace, become peace yourself."*

The teachings of Tibetan Buddhism are, in this respect, very subtle. They remind us that at the moment of death, your senses—and the very powerful but incomplete information they send you—dissolve along with everything that contributes to the construction of the illusion of "me." This includes your emotions, thoughts, and feeling of identity, from which you derive the impression of being something independent of the rest, something permanent and solid. Once the "drop of consciousness" has ceased, there is only a short moment before you come into your true nature, the infinite nonlocal consciousness, the ocean of consciousness.

How does a soul identify this and stay there? It is a matter of recognizing it, which is possible if you have already experienced it during life. This is "illumination," and it is for this reason that death is one of the most precious events of existence. But beware: Although all this dismantling of the senses and the ordinary mind at the end of life occurs for everyone, including animals, the nonlocal consciousness manifests itself fully only for a quick moment for each person, just before the ordinary consciousness can be rebuilt for an afterlife. You will only be able to benefit from it if you are capable of being consciously aware of yourself, of recognizing what you have already known during life and consciously living your own death.

Of all the training of the spirit in which the Tibetans engage, I can only recommend this: It is never too early to start!

For a list of the writings of Daniela Muggia, published in French, see the end of this book.

Laurence Guillaumie *(professor at Université Laval in Quebec, director of a Buddhist center)*

(July 23, 2017, Quebec) Before putting on paper how I envision death and the after-death, it seems to me necessary first to express in words what Life is.

Life appears to me as an energetic, conscious, and mysterious totality. Paradoxically, we can attribute to Life all the qualifying adjectives and none. She is everything, the full and the empty, the feminine and the masculine, the immanence and the transcendence, the existent and the nonexistent. Life manifests herself in different forms and in different realms (animal, vegetable, mineral, etc.). Each person is a manifestation or expression of life in the human realm. But above all, it is important to say that each person is a creative consciousness, and that is what characterizes the human realm.

Each person inevitably unfolds his or her creative consciousness, his own "science," his "knowledge," or his "vision" of Life, which is manifested by his thoughts, emotions, and actions. This "science" of each person can be identified as being Life herself, but it can also totally ignore this dimension and recognize itself essentially in the ego, by identifying itself with a physical body and consisting of a set of cultural, familial, and personal impressions and conditioning.

Each person is therefore a creative consciousness that can be situated in the paradigm of being a person, being Life, or somewhere in between. It is remarkable that the person who creates from the ego and identifies with the illusion of being a person cannot, however, divest himself or degrade his true nature of being Life.

The person is Life but forgets this by experiencing personality instead of being.

In the paradigm of the ego, there is a push to succeed and goals to achieve to be finally good, kind, happy, sufficient, appropriate, and so on. The ego is scared, worried, and constantly seeking improvement in the hope of ultimate felicity.

In the paradigm of Life, you are already Life, you are already Love, and you are already the Light. As the great sages have said, the good news is that you are already Life itself, and this is the meaning of the Annunciation. Everyone is already what they are looking for. The "sins" are already forgiven.

The person who does not identify with the ego continues to have an ego nevertheless and to feel inclinations. This person then acts and creates according to those inclinations. The creative conscience plays with enthusiasm the game of being human and creating its own human manifestation.

213

From there, we can ask: Are we ready, at this very moment, to abandon this identification with the limited and imperfect "little self"? The answer is no, for most of us. The problem—if there is a problem—is loyalty to identifying as a "person" and attaching to the "little stories of little people."

At present, one can look at human death as it unfolds from the point of view of ego or Life. The ego tells all kinds of stories about itself, including the meaning of existence and death. The ego imagines its death as the end and destruction of the person.

From the point of view of Life, death takes a different form. Life is without beginning or end. Death is not an end but a transition. Likewise, birth is not a beginning, strictly speaking, but rather an arrival and a departure. Logically, it is nonsense to think that Life would be worried about death. On the contrary, for the ego, death is a total loss.

To more deeply understand what death is from the point of view of Life, close your eyes and leave aside for a moment all your identifications and concepts as a person. There is no longer an "I see" but a "see." The evidence is that Life takes care of herself and does what she has to do. Existential questions about death dissipate. Life has her own plans for each person and for humanity. Life likes to disappear and reappear. If a death occurs, it means that it had to happen.

Once these foundations are laid, two fundamental questions are revealed with regard to death and the postdeath period, for which I find that I have no vision.

What logic of Life determines births and deaths, manifestations and transformations? What are the implications of dying identified with the idea of being a person? These topics are among the subtlest and most mysterious.

It can be assumed that your conception of Life and death strongly determines what death can look like. As the gospels say, "There are many dwelling places in my Father's house."

My understanding of the phenomena of death and postdeath is modest. What counts for me is to remember that we are Life, to live in harmony with everything inside and outside of us, and to laugh. What is laughter if not an affectionate expression of Life itself?

Olivier Boiral *(professor at Université Laval in Quebec, author of many scientific articles)*

Death is a process of transformation and a recomposing of different elements or aggregates that make up the Living during an incarnation and of which the life duration does not necessary coincide with the physical body existence. *Thinking about death leads one to wonder what dying means fundamentally with regard to the components that define our being.*

To manifest, your spiritual essence needs different "bodies" or envelopes, more or less dense, that condition your relative experience of reality and act as prisms by which the undifferentiated Light of the Divine expresses itself. This is creative, colorful, changing, and unique for each of us in the grand theater of life.

The Hindus speak about five main *Koshas*, or envelopes, that comprise the true nature (the Brahman), both immanent and transcendent, of everything. Although these envelopes are inextricably linked, much like in a system of Russian nesting dolls, they do not all have the same fate at the moment of death. The identification of the individual with some of the Koshas can significantly influence the path of his or her soul postmortem.

The fates of the first two envelopes, the physical body *(Annamaya Kosha)* and the ethereal body *(Pranamaya Kosha)*, are not unclear. They dissolve in their respective elements and will serve to nourish other forms of life because everything is transformed in nature, life constantly feeding on death.

The fates of the subtler envelopes are more complex, more uncertain, and more controversial, even within spiritual traditions. Therefore, I am only presenting my understanding, which is necessarily limited by inexperience with death—I'm still living!—which, I hope, you will not hold against me.

In short, I believe that the other subtler envelopes that make up and shape one's individuality survive physical death, but *they are not immortal*, since they continually transform by offering their experiences to the Spirit or *Atman* (the Divine) within individual incarnated beings.

On our very small human scale, we can say that this field of the Divine and Universal Consciousness is eternal. However, I believe, at a much larger scale, it is subject to creative transformation, and each individual is involved with his or her unique vibration.

The emotional or astral body *(Manomaya Kosha)* is the most unstable of all. It constantly changes color (which we call the "aura"), and although it survives physical death, it is continually transformed by the vicissitudes of existence, including the moment of death.

The mental body *(Vijnanamaya Kosha)*, which is the seat of intelligence, discrimination, and wisdom, is subtler, deeper, and full blown, which results from many experiences or incarnations and a more refined comprehension of our true nature. It seeks to correctly identify the densest envelopes, mostly those attached to the physical body and emotions.

In the very long term, the astral body and the mental body will know a kind of death independent from the physical body. In any case, I believe that their essence will be somehow "absorbed" into the "Body of Beatitude," which itself will end by melting totally into the Divine, to which it is constantly connected.

Although the Body of Beatitude *(Anandamaya Kosha)* is the most precious and independent in the embodied ego, paradoxically there are few clear things written about it, perhaps because it remains rather undeveloped in most of us and so its existence may seem mysterious or even abstract.

Intense happiness, mystical ecstasies *(samādhi)*, deep joy, and unconditional love contribute gradually to nourishing, stimulating, and reinforcing this Body of Beatitude also called the "Body of Glory."

The continuous establishment of human consciousness in the *Anandamaya Kosha* is, I believe, the more or less conscious foundation of any true mystical quest. Even short experiences of *samādhi* (intense concentration) bring an orgasmic state of unity to the apparent diversity in reality and tend to gradually leave conditioning imprints *(samskāras)* that influence one's successive rebirths *(samsāra)*. These imprints act like "mental programs" permanently projected onto the screen of consciousness during your life in the Afterlife.

In nourishing the Anandamaya Kosha, such an ecstatic experience brings joy to one's pure state and eliminates the fear of death, which has no influence on the Divine Essence.

The purpose of life and death is to develop the Body of Beatitude within and around you. The Body of Beatitude is the "asset" that enables you to get in and out of the physical world. It's an asset you choose to care for with heart-centered actions and your acceptance of life. I am thinking here of the Parable of the Talents in the Bible.

In this context, in my opinion, the process of death (including what follows after the detachment of the physical body) cannot be predetermined, monolithic, and identical for all. This process depends on a person's identification with the different envelopes, level of development of the subtlest Koshas, past actions, and also inner state at the time of death.

For example, death no longer really exists for a being who has experienced deep mystical states. If it happens at the time of such an experience, the being will certainly be liberated, without any possible return toward differentiation and identification with the more superficial envelopes.

In the meantime, and for the majority of us, I believe that death can be seen as a sort of "moving out" of the soul, like a change of residence or anchorage point of the aggregate formed by the complex interactions of the subtle envelopes *(the Manomaya Kosha, Vijnanamaya Kosha, and Anandamaya Kosha)*.

This moving out can be difficult sometimes, even exhausting and scary. For most, it takes a variable duration of time to reach a subtler—but just as illusory—vibratory level resonating with one's deep being, karma, and the family of souls to which one is bound.

Like a lot of moves, we often take with us too many things and useless old memories. Personally, I hope to travel as lightly as possible, and freely. Although the address of our future home is not known for most of us, we can hope that the place is happy, bright, and warm, and as far as possible from the sad, dark, sentententious, and cold atmosphere of a burial.

I also imagine a dwelling place where we can continue to learn and share without being forced to return to Earth. Contrary to the romantic speeches on reincarnation, the vast majority of new births are currently in overcrowded and polluted places, which are not always conducive to the free development of the being.

Imagining what happens after death may seem futile or puerile, but it may also be a deeper exercise than it seems because one's beliefs and vision of things tend to shape one's universe, especially on the subtle planes of the Afterlife.

In this context, believing that you are simply a mortal body and identifying with it tends to enslave you, predisposing you to the fear of death and distancing you from its great initiatory power. Truly identifying with your deep nature and establishing yourself in the Body of Beatitude at the moment of death liberate you. Between these two extremes, most humans imagine death based on dogmas and predefined beliefs that could very well shape without their knowledge what will become their experiences beyond the grave.

For a list of the writings of Olivier Boiral, published in French, see the end of this book.

Annabelle de Villedieu *(psychic medium, clairvoyant, Marseille Tarot readings)*

Since my sweet childhood, I've had a gift. I'm a psychic medium/clairvoyant with a hypersensitivity that allows me to see the world in a different way. Flashes of images of great precision accompanied by a subtle feeling impose themselves on me.

Though I was brought up in a family environment closed to spirituality, I always believed in reincarnation as an intrinsic truth and felt myself belonging to another space-time. I could not find my place in this world that I saw as impure! I was led, along the way, to discover that I must truly embody my physical body to fully realize the mission of my soul.

All my painful past-life experiences have taught me that I must extract the best moments from them and that I must accept and transmute them into the Great Mind. This is a part of the learning process of liberating my soul from heavy memories and moving beyond them. The first manifestations of my psychic abilities came with death. At the age of eight, one of my aunts physically appeared to me at the moment of her departure. I had not seen her for years, and I described her so precisely that my parents were shocked.

At the age of nine, a member of my family was hospitalized. I felt his death, and a smell of decay filled my nostrils. I was also able to give the exact time that he passed. Every time there was a death of someone I knew, I heard cries and was invaded by obsessional ideas of death. I didn't understand what was happening to me. As soon as the person left, I felt liberated!

At the age of thirteen, after visiting my sexagenarian grandfather, I was certain that I would not see him again. I had such a sobering dream of his death that I remained deeply marked. Sadly, three months later, I learned of his death. At the same time, I was entering a path of initiation.

At the age of fourteen, in love with the Sacred Heart of Jesus, I heard in my ear messages of love and teachings from other levels of consciousness.

Then, at seventeen, I found my grandmother dead in her bed. In front of her inert body, I realized that her physical body was just a frame for her soul because I felt her presence energetically. The next night, she visited me. I saw her and heard her talking to me about her son, with whom she'd lived.

She shared with me intimate messages so precise that my uncle knew they were from her.

At eighteen, I fell into a semicoma following a virus. It seemed I was leaving, and I began to abandon myself to the infinite and subtle preciousness of life.

At twenty, my father fell into a coma and returned after a clinical death experience. He told me that he had not wanted to come back and that he was not afraid anymore because on the Other Side, "Everything is light and beauty."

At twenty-two, I met a master of Sufi Hinduism who'd gathered all the spiritual paths into one—the path of the Universal. I followed his teachings for five years.

Finally, at the age of thirty-three, after being an engineer in the aeronautical industry and attending an art school, life removed all I had! I heard an inner call that said, "Now it's time to accept your mission."

I said yes and chose to accompany and guide beings to realization. Beyond seeing the past, the present, and the future to help incarnate souls, I regularly come in contact with disembodied souls who transmit messages to me. I also accompany these souls into the Light.

On this path, I discovered shamanism. In my travels, during which I am in a modified state of consciousness naturally, I connect with beings from different planes of consciousness and receive messages from my Guides of Light.

With the help of hallucinogenic plants from the jungle, I experience the modified states of consciousness as well as my own death, an ecstatic passage where I meet the Unity and the Unlimited. I see myself above my physical body and breathe in all the cells of my Body of Light. I am the totality part of the All. I have trouble coming back because my body limits me.

A little later, I experimented unintentionally with an astral journey. I saw myself leaving my body, dying, and I entered a vibratory space where the beings are only forms of energy. I was attracted by some I recognized, like a magnet, and repulsed by others. I returned to my physical body with a lot of pain.

One day, an amazing experience happened to me! I picked up a small bird that had fallen to the ground. I took it in my hands and sent him energy. He came back to life, and then suddenly I felt myself fainting, coming out of my body, just as he died in my hand. Then I followed the path of Tantra Yoga and experienced the kundalini energy by walking across death, an orgasmic passage during which my body expanded to touch beatitude, unconditional love, and unity.

Then came the death of my father. I had been busy and didn't see him near the end. I felt physically pained deep in my heart when he passed. So I understand! During the wake for my father, I felt unconditional love empowering me to see that everything is possible when hearts are connected. So much peace!

His presence (due to his odor) expressed a certain time. One night, he visited me to tell me that everything is Light, and I received this energy of pure love. He has not visited since that moment!

Then three years later, my mother's death came. I accompanied her through ten hours of agony and received her fear of dying. She had too much unfinished business and too many earthly attachments! I was suddenly invaded by the energy of the Divine Mother to help my mom make the passage into forgiveness. It was a wonderful gift, but a part of me left with her.

Six months passed, and I found myself on the verge of death with a hemorrhage, which my mother had died from. At this moment, I returned to the full consciousness of death. I understood that my incarnated life is but a piece of my energetic identity, which contains all the memories of my previous lives.

I was then connected to the Universal Consciousness, and I found my vibratory totality. I merged with higher planes of consciousness that resonated with my own vibration at the moment of my departure. I understood that I came to be incarnate to purify myself of my karmic memories and to live the magnificent experience of the Presence. I consciously chose my terrestrial family in order to find my soul family: the light beings with undefined, elongated, white humanoid forms who infuse me with the energy of love. I felt fully welcomed in the Unconditional Consciousness and its lightness.

I came back then and looked at the material world with much detachment, in that nothing belongs to me. Everything is ephemeral because I'm only crossing this temporality.

No more attachments. No more possessions. No more wanting. This brush with death enabled me to learn how to consciously enjoy what life offers me every moment. Everything is in the consciousness!

So I thank my body that allows me to experience the beauty, the richness, and the density of the material—touching, smelling, creating, breathing, loving.

For me, life and death are at every moment in the movement of creation. Everything is summed up with the inhale and the exhale. Everything is impermanence in the permanence. Death as an end does not exist!

Martine Pascalet *(collaborator of Daniel Meurois, editorial manager of the former Editions Amrita)*

(Spring 2017) How do I envision my death? This is a question I did not think I had to answer during my lifetime!

But since it is presented, I cannot turn my back on it. I must face this question, even though it leaves me perplexed at first.

What comes to mind spontaneously is that I would like to have a peaceful departure, one not due to an accident or a deadly disease, so my loved ones who remain will experience as little pain as possible.

I say "departure," but I could just as easily use the words "death" or "end of life." However, those connote a break more difficult than just a departure. It will be a trip to another life, it seems to me.

Yes, I envisage a peaceful and free end of life. I want to be able to tell myself that I have accomplished my mission, knowing that behind me and after me, everything concerning me will be settled in a clear way, without constraint or obligations for those who stay.

I would like for all of my loved ones to smile upon hearing the news of my departure. Toward this goal, I will put all my heart into making each one of them quickly feel my invisible presence with a little breath or a sign, like the one I received from one of my friends during his funeral in a small church one winter morning.

I do not want to see the people I love suffer.

Even though most of them are aware that death is not an end in itself, it is hard to escape our emotions. Ah! Emotions that upset you so much are one of the biggest traps in life.

When I leave the liberated mind and fly lightly, some efforts will await me as I finish with my known and unknown weaknesses and work to reinforce my good attitudes
- Still divest myself
- Still grow up
- Still smile
- Still serve
- Still thank
- Still forgive
- Still love more

Do I still have time in this lifetime, or do I have to be ready right away?

If I'm lingering too long in my life on this Earth, I know a sister-friend, with her amused, sparkling, and deep eyes, will be at my side upon my departure to walk with me into the Passage and connect me with my loved ones, those of my soul family, on the Other Side.

Friends, brothers, sisters—forever united by the same indestructible link.

I will thank the Guides and Beings of Light for their patience and benevolence, and they will share with me teachings that will awaken me again and again, that will expand my heart again and again. And perhaps, if it's possible, I will meet and thank Master Yeshua and receive His teachings, a blessing of His love and light.

In order to never forget.

In order to know how to give back what I will have received.

Finally, to BE.

Do these few lines testify to a dream, an illusion, or an intuition?

Will this become reality? I wish I could tell you, as much as I wish I could live it. Only a few will be able to testify to the first part (of my life).

Marie Johanne Croteau-Meurois *(author, editor, psychic medium, therapist-teacher, end-of-life coach, Helper Soul)*

Here, I will share how I envision my own death and afterlife. But first, I will quote the simple and exact words of Sage Purusha to introduce such a reflection: "The human no longer knows how to die."

Yes, it is true that human beings have unlearned what all beings have been able to do naturally for millennia. This is why I think it is important to ask this fundamental question and to have a glimpse of the coming of such a moment in full awareness and without anxiety or panic. Because, whether you like it or not, you are mortal, and the hour of departure will come.

Talking about death is scary and may seem like a winding way to get closer to it, or rather bring it closer to you. I think about death every day. I look at her, and I tame her because I know her "after." I know she is there, a certainty because of my human flesh condition, but I also know from my experience that the end of this condition will not mean the end of my being.

This "after"—I go through it because I live it in my flesh. This book is a testament to it. I regularly visit the "Beyond" to help the deceased, and I come back. Death—I know her from within. Such a gift—or peculiarity, if you prefer—is very strange, but it is a teacher and opens great doors to the multiple worlds that exist around us and in us.

What I hope is to not die after my children because it is humanly illogical for a parent to leave after a child. This is, in my opinion, too great a test of life, though it happens to many people for many reasons. I would also like as much as possible not to end my life bedridden, senile, with dementia, or suffering too much. I already have an idea of how my passing will be. But I am keeping this secret to myself.

I also know where I will go. I know who will come for me. And I know who I will join. I will find a beloved Grand Master and my family of souls and animal friends, and I will also welcome those who will join me one day (my children and several friends found in this life). For sure, we all are scheduled to meet in specific spaces of our common visions, those of the "ideal paradise" of the heart. This "interior territory" is linked to the colors of the soul and to the continuation of one's work in the Beyond but also to the preparation for our return because we will come back, my dear ones and myself, to continue our mission of helping humanity and growing too until the moment of the Great Awakening.

As I write these lines, I can say that I am in the autumn of my life. I am aware of this, but I also know that around 2030 to 2050, there will be a lot more to do. So, I'll come back without waiting too long. Daniel, my husband, and I are currently talking about this subject and our likely future terrestrial commitments.

At the appropriate time, I will give specific instructions for how to prepare my old clothing of flesh in terms of essential burial rituals for the facilitation of the Passage. All the elements will be indicated in my last wishes.

Those who are classically trained in the West do not respect the basic and important laws that are imposed after the rupture of the silver cord binding the soul and the body, which initiates the departure of the vital energies of the body of the deceased.

It is not that I attach a particular importance to the flesh, but the more I know of the principles that need to be respected so that the soul is born gently into the Beyond, the more I believe certain gestures are required as a person takes his or her last breath.

As for the birth of a newborn, which must also happen smoothly, this "birth of Heaven" has its own requirements in agreement, of course, with the beliefs and wishes of the deceased.

One's human status necessitates respecting some universal laws to avoid serious discomfort when "in transit" (or crossing over) to the Other Side. Because analogically, I would say that nobody likes to hang out in corridors or in a passageway.

Such precautions, these marks of respect, are also valid for funerals. Embalming or not, incineration or burial, grave or urn, or nothing at all, as well as purifying flowers and oils— these are not necessarily just details, believe me. Some souls attach real importance to them.

Of course, there are differences between people, races, and kingdoms too. Animals have their own very discrete rituals and call their guiding souls, their "Devas," to assist them in grief.

In another book, I wrote about death among the elves, the people of the air element. For them, death is a logical continuation of a long existence of service to life, and it simply happens like a leaf in autumn, falling from a tree in a flutter. I dream of this sometimes as a kind of ideal, expressed by the lines below:

"The elven soul, you see, holds both the animal soul and the human soul in what they spontaneously express. There exists a kind of harmonious and light marriage between both; however, this union is fundamentally amoral, without any intention but to sustain and extend the sacred Breath of Life. There is no religion and no dogma, only the permanent life of necessary service to the sacred wave from which the soul came. No discussion and no doubt exist in this respect" (The Portal of the Elves by Marie Johanne Croteau-Meurois).

226

To return to my present condition, that of being a human, I'm not worried about my death but rather how I'm going to die. I do not worry because I know there is a wonderful Sun of Light that awaits us all, without exception, where we can rest and recharge our batteries. When you carry this sun in your heart and it feeds you, you will certainly find it quickly after death. The predictable approach of the departure from Earth invites you to examine your conscience and visualize the important passages of your journey. So, I know that I have to continue my reflections—reflections that, I believe, everyone should conduct with honesty and compassion as the years begin to accumulate. While doing this, it's important that you not feel guilty but instead "clean up your place a bit" and see more clearly. Ask questions like these: How did you act? What were your good and bad acts? What do you need to work on over and over again in order to be a better soul and move faster toward your supreme flowering, that of your return to the Source?

On the Other Side, no one will condemn you. You will be your only judge. With the help of your Devachan guides, you will incarnate according to your "heavenly bank account" or karma, when it is time to experience life on Earth again and work on what is still unfinished in the soul.

I've read several books containing the following words: "The soul is eternal. It does not die." That is not exactly correct. Certainly, the soul does not die with the body of flesh because it has experienced thousands of lives and will experience many more until everything in it has become a pure diamond, that of your Quintessence. The soul will blend with her twin flame, her other self, her masculine and feminine unified to become a single, purely cosmic flame ready to go back to the Creator, the Breath, the Divine. There are many names for this, all referring to the same principle.

This is why I invite you to think of your celestial home now so that the fear of death will fade away and be replaced by a gentle teacher, revealing to you how to transmute your vibrations ever higher.

For a list of the writings of Marie Johanne Croteau-Meurois, published in English, see the end of this book.

Notes and References

Dr. Jean-Jacques Charbonnier *is an anesthetist-resuscitator. Still working, he has been studying near-death experiences for thirty years. A member of the French Intensive Care Society and author of several books on this subject, he gives conferences worldwide.*

Bibliography: "La mort décodée" 2008, "La médecine face à l'au-delà" 2010, "Les 7 bonnes raisons de croire à l'au-delà" 2012, "Les 3 clés pour vaincre les pires épreuves de la vie" 2013, "4 regards sur la mort et ses tabous" 2015, "La mort expliquée aux enfants" 2016, "La conscience intuitive extraneuronale" 2017 – Ed. Guy Trédaniel. "Les preuves scientifiques d'une vie après la vie 2008, Ed. Chez Exergue. "Histoires incroyables d'un anesthesiste reanimateur" 2010, Ed. Au Cherche Midi "Cette chose..." 2017 Ed. Chez First.

Laila Del Monte *(medium-therapist for the animal soul, author, and teacher in Spain, France, and North America [Canada and the U.S.])*

Bibliography: http://lailadelmonte.com/en/

"Psychic Communication with Animals for Health and Healing" in Amazon, "Les animaux...leur chemin vers l'autre monde" (Animals –their journey to the other side), "Quand le

*cheval guide l'homme" (When the horse guides the human" –
Three books publishing in Editions Vega.*

Dr. Eric Dudoit *(Ph.D. in psychology, theologian, author,
teacher in the School of Medicine in Aix-en-Provence, hospice
practitioner in the Hospital of La Timone in Marseille, and
founder of the Clinic of Spirit)*

Bibliography: *Le cancer au coeur du spiritual (Cancer at the
heart of spirituality) Ed. S17: Ces E.M.I qui nous soignent
(These NDE who heal us), La Porte à franchir (The Door to
cross) Ed Le Passe-Monde.*

Dr. Guy Londechamp *(doctor and researcher in energy
medicine)*

Bibliography: *La Symphonie du vivant (The Symphony of
the living) Editions Miexon 1987 (out of stock) – L'Homme
vibratoire (The vibrational Human) – Editions Amrita
(France) 1991 second edition in 1998 (out of stock as well).
Guy Longdechamp is particularly involved in research work
on water since 2007 because it is at the heart of biological
life and any integral vision of health (vortex systems, clinical
tests with the pulse, sensitive crystallizations, tests with the
Korotkov's camera).*

Mark Vallée *(editor and founder of Ariane Editions, author,
and lecturer)*

Bibliography: *Pionnier de l'Eveil (Pioneer of Awakening) –
Editions Ariane. http://editions-ariane.com/*

Annie Lautner (*author and poet*)

*Annie Lautner is an author, poet, and philosopher. It has been
said that her words touch, lift up, serve as a resource, open,*

invite, comfort, call to mind, and reveal. She lives and writes in Alsace (www.annie-lautner.com).

Johanne Razanamahay *(shaman, author, and teacher)*

Bibliography: *La mort n'est pas un accident (Death is not an accident), Voyage vers les spheres celestes (Voyage towards the celestian spheres) Editions Lanore, www.santeglobale.com*

Marie-Chantal Martineau *(author, artist-illustrator, medium-therapist, teacher of the Angelic Tianshi therapies)*

Bibliography: *Mon album d'adoption (My album of adoption) 2010 – Mon album de bébé (My album of baby) 201 – l"Oracle de l'Ame intuitive (The Oracle of the Intuitive Soul) 2014 with collaboration with Lisa Williams – L'Oracle Angelique (The Angelic Oracle) 2015 –Inspirations angeliques (Angelic Inspirations) 2015 – Les Anges, tels que je les vois (Angels as I see Them) 2016 – Pour ceux qui restent (For the ones who stay) 2017. All these titles are published in French in Editions Le Dauphin Blanc. www.dauphinblanc.com*

Alain Williamson *(founder and CEO of Éditions Le Dauphin Blanc, editor, author, trainer, and translator)*

Bibliography: *Le tableau de vie (The painting of life), 2012 – Le manuel pratique du tableau de vie, 2012 (The handbook of the painting of life), 2012 – Le carnet de vie (The notebook of life), 2012 – Le calepin de David Marteens (David Marteens's notebook) 2013 – Le Luthier (The stringed instrument maker) 2013 – Agenda annuel (Annual agenda) 2015-2016-2017-2018) – La villa des miracles (The villa of miracles) 2014 – Ho'oponopono, 2015 – La chamane d'Ek-Balam (The shaman of Ek-Balam) 2016 – Miracles 2016 in collaboration with Annick Lapratte – Les cinq codes d'eveil (The fifth codes of awakening) 2017 www.dauphinblanc.com*

Hélène Giroux *(author and end-of-life coach)*

Hélène Giroux has been passionate about people for a long time, and her desire to contribute to the evolution of consciousness has always guided her choices. An experience with a dying aunt transformed her life, and after being trained as a "beneficiary," she finally chose to work with people at the end of their lives. Interested in helping the public by demystifying death, she has since participated in continuing education, gives lectures, writes articles, and is the author of three books on the subject. This vocation gives meaning to her life.

Bibliography*: Le privilège d'accompagner...choisir la mort (The privilege to accompany by choosing death) Ed. La Plume d'Oie, 2012 – Ce que les mourants m'ont enseigné (What the dying people taught me); L'apprentissage de la vie au seuil de la mort (Learning about life on the brink of death) –Ed, Le Dauphin Blanc, 2015 – Accompagner... guide essential pour une présence en fin de vie (To Accompany – Essential guidance for a presence at the end of life) Ed Le Dauphin Blanc, 2016 www://helenegiroux.com www.facebook.com/accompagnementsetsoins*

Sophie Andrieu *(president of Women in Action, pioneer of humanitarian aid, channeling medium, and author)*

Bibliography*: Le testament de l'âme (The Legacy of the soul) coming soon, Ed. Arianne. Sophieu Audrieu is also an ambassador for the Humanitarian Aid at the United Nations and initiator of the collective "Human in Action" which unified more than three hundred therapists, writers, philosophers, lecturers and scientists to act against the global warming and the protection of the environment. In 2011, she decided to act on a larger scale in the heart of the Sacred Feminine and created a female SCOP* in the Moroccan desert: more than two hundred women are now autonomous.*

* Cooperative and Participative Society which can be compare to a Cooperative or Coop in USA.

Daniela Muggia *(editor, Edizioni Amrita, Italy; teacher of end-of-life coaching; speaker; and author)*

Biobligraphy*: Daniela Muggia is the author of several articles and co-author of two books first published in Italian. One of her books dedicated to the ECEL method in the approach of the suffering of the living persons in this case children with ADHD, is already translated in Spanish (Los Jaimitos, Ni Tocarlos! Acompañamentos empático de los niños que padecen TDAH) and in English (The Impact of Empathy – A New Approach to Working with ADHD Children (Attention Deficit Hyperactivity Disorder) at Blossoming Books.*

The other book dedicated to the end of life accompaniment of animals (Tenersi per zampa fino alla fine) exists in Spanish (Mano con Pata hasta el Final – Acompañamiento empático y cuidado paliativo para los animals al final de la vida) and will appear soon in English (Paw in Hand Until the End: Empathic and Palliative Care at the End of Life for Pets) at Blossoming Books and French at Amrita.

A third book is in preparation dedicated to her twenty-five experience next to those she considers to be her greatest masters: the dying themselves.

References, articles and videos in English: www.danielamuggia.it

Contact in French and English: info@danielamuggia.it

Also available to consult:
http://it.linkedin.com/pub/Daniela-muggia/ab/b16/b14
http:independent.academia.edu/danielamuggia

Olivier Boiral *(professor at Université Laval in Quebec and author of many scientific articles)*

Olivier Boiral has been interested in spiritual issues and has practiced meditation for over thirty-five years. In the 1990s, he was a yoga teacher and became interested in Indian spiritual traditions, especially Advaita Vedanta and Shaivism from Kashmir. More recently, he attended training in the Essenian and Egyptian therapies. A professor at a great Canadian university in Quebec City, he has published hundreds of scientific articles, books, and chapters on sustainable development related to the rise of human consciousness.

Marie-Johanne Croteau-Meurois *(author, editor, psychic medium, therapist-teacher, end-of-life coach, Helper Soul)*

Bibliography: *The Great Book of the Essenian and Egyptian therapies (in collaboration with Daniel Meurois) – The Portal of the Elves, memories from elsewhere – These Souls who leave us, twelve stories from the Afterlife. Three books published in Sacred Worlds Publishing.*

After practicing as a pharmacist in the trauma department of a large hospital center, Marie Johanne Croteau-Meurois is now a publisher, producer of events, author, psychic medium, therapist-teacher, and Soul Walker.
intusolaris@ccpabable.com
www.intus-solaris.com
www.esseniens.com

Glossary

Being extra sensory: Being not limited to this dimension or time-space reality.

Devachan: This universe will reveal itself totally in agreement with their deep aspirations, their ideal. It is useful to specify, then, that the Devachan is also the vibratory result of a multitude of sensitivities, and so it is composed of many worlds.

Egregore: An autonomous psychic entity made up of, and influencing, the thoughts of a group of people.

Helper Soul : The Helper Soul, also called the Walker, helps lost souls or souls with difficult deaths at the crossover. Also know as "Walkers between the worlds" by the Ancient Greek Philosophers, these gifted people can step into the other side of the veil to help a dead one to make the final steps toward The Light or Heaven. They can walk to a certain limit into the Afterlife and come back to our physical world.

Kamaloca :

It is a space where souls reproduce their terrestrial functioning schemas with all their limitations. In this state, they are not necessarily aware of "having crossed the border" or going around in circles tirelessly.

Silver Cord:

The Silver Cord is made of etheric matter. "Yes, remember your Creator now while you are young, before the silver cord of life snaps and the golden bowl is broken." — Ecclesiastes 12:6 The silver cord is an energetic umbilicus connecting both the physical and subtle bodies. It stays in tact for the duration of a person's physical life. Upon death the silver cord is broker and the soul is released to travel to the Other Side of the Veil.

End Notes

1. Being hypersensitive means not being limited to this dimension or time-space reality.

2. Near-death experience.

3. "Helper Soul" is the one who helps souls stuck in crossover.

4. *Il y a de Nombreuses Demeures: À la Découverte des Univers Parallèles* (There Are Many Dwelling Places: Discovering the Parallel Worlds) by Daniel Meurois, Ed. Le Passe-Monde.

5. *Il y a de Nombreuses Demeures: À la Découverte des Univers Parallèles* (There Are Many Dwelling Places: Discovering the Parallel Worlds) by Daniel Meurois, Ed. Le Passe-Monde.

6. *Le Testament des Trois Marie* (Legacy of the Three Marys) by Daniel Meurois, Ed. Le Passe-Monde.

7. *Le Peuple Animal* (The Animal People : The Souls of the Animals) by Daniel Meurois, Ed Le Passe-Monde.

8. *The Great Book of Essenian & Egyptian Therapies* by Marie Johanne Croteau and Daniel Meurois, Ed. Sacred Worlds Publishing.

9. "Jo" was an affectionate nickname that my relatives gave me.

10. Jackman is a town in Somerset County in the state of Maine in the United States. It is the last municipality in the US before you reach the Canadian border. The closest hospital is one hour away, in a small town called Skowhegan.

11. The out-of-body experience easily allows me, in my Body of Light, to touch the dead, and they too can feel my body, which reassures them.

12. A kind of energetic psychic bubble created by a person who died violently.

13. As we have already seen, a sudden death is difficult to accept for the person who is leaving. She finds herself in a place where she does not understand the internal logic. Her bearings are upset due to her not being prepared. Unable to communicate, she feels lost because she mixes together all the last moments of her life and repeats them to herself over and over again until she moves through the next transition.

14. *Le Non désiré* (The Unwanted) by Daniel Meurois, Ed. Le Passe-Monde.

15. *The Great Book of Essenian & Egyptian Therapies* by Marie Johanne Croteau and Daniel Meurois, Ed. Sacred Worlds Publishing.

16. *Les Familles d'Âmes* (Soul Families) by Marie Lise Labonté.

17. *Le Non désiré* (The Unwanted) by Daniel Meurois, Ed. Le Passe-Monde.

18. "In this state of out of the body... the individual feels cut off from others. He is able to see others and to fully penetrate their thoughts, but on the other hand they cannot see him or hear him. All communication with human beings is in fact suspended, even at the level of touch, when the spiritual body lacks solidity. Therefore, we will not be astonished if, when this state lasts a certain time, the individual ends up experiencing a profound loneliness" (*Life After Life* by Dr. Raymond Moody).

19. *Ce Clou que J'ai enfoncé* (This Nail That I Have Hammered) by Daniel Meurois, Ed. Le Passe-Monde.

20. *La mort n'est jamais un accident* (Death Is Never an Accident) by Johanne Razanamahay.

21. "I have been able to discuss very openly... with people suffering from interferences at the level of identity. They always ask me whether the fragility and permeability characterizing them could have karmic origins. These

questions can only be answered on a case-by-case basis. Indeed, many events in a life, especially in childhood or adolescence, are enough to explain such disorders. Do not use karma, or 'acute karma,' as a solution for everything" (*Les Maladies Karmiques* (The Karmic Diseases) by Daniel Meurois).

22. *Le Non désiré* (The Unwanted) by Daniel Meurois, Ed. Le Passe-Monde.

23. *Ce Clou que J'ai enfoncé* (This Nail That I Have Hammered) by Daniel Meurois, Ed. Le Passe-Monde.

24. See Chapter One, "The Choice of Simone".

25. *Ce qu'Ils m'ont dit* (What They Told Me) by Daniel Meurois, Ed. Le Passe-Monde.

26. The silver cord made of etheric matter.

27. *Chronique d'un départ afin de guider ceux qui nous quittent* (Chronicle of a Departure to Help Those Who Leave Us) by Daniel Meurois and Anne Givaudan, Ed. Le Passe-Monde.

28. In French, "Dominique" is a name used for both genders.

29. Near-death experience.

30. Near-death experiences are reported by an estimated 200,000 Americans a year, and studies around the world suggest NDEs are a common human experience (by Tara MacIsaac, The Epoch Times, June 2014).

31. *Journey of Souls* by Michael Newton.

32. *Il y a de Nombreuses Demeures: À la Découverte des Univers Parallèles* (There Are Many Dwelling Places: Discovering the Parallel Worlds) by Daniel Meurois. ed. Le Passe-Monde.

33. gdvcamera.com

34. The "explosion of water drops" refers metaphorically to how the body, at the time of death, returns the water it

contains to the world. A person who is dying shows a significant increase in dryness. Without water, a person may only survive for few days.

35. Collective group mind. An autonomous psychic entity made up of, and influencing, the thoughts of a group of people (Wikipedia).

36. Near-death experience.

37. Dead or Not? The Last Medical Discoveries of the N.D.E. (INREES).

Also By

Sacred Worlds Publishing
www.sacredworldspublishing.com

Our books reveal timeless wisdom to awaken
and empower the soul.

The Great Book of Essenian & Egyptian Therapies
A must read for all body workers
looking to deepen and expand their practice.

The Portal of the Elves
Memories from Elsewhere
A true tale of harmony and freedom
between lifetimes and realms.

Made in the USA
Lexington, KY
26 November 2019